Liberty
and
Hard Cases

*The Hoover Institution
gratefully acknowledges
the support of*

JOANNE AND JOHAN BLOKKER

on this project.

PHILOSOPHIC REFLECTIONS ON A FREE SOCIETY

Liberty
and
Hard Cases

Edited by
Tibor R. Machan

HOOVER INSTITUTION PRESS

Stanford University   Stanford, California

www.hoover.org

Hoover Institution Press Publication No. 492
Copyright © 2002 by the Board of Trustees of the
Leland Stanford Junior University

First printing 2002
08   07   06   05   04   03   02   9   8   7   6   5   4   3   2   1

Manufactured in the United States of America
The paper used in this publication meets the minimum requirements
of American National Standard for Information Sciences—Permanence
of Paper for Printed Library Materials, ANSI Z39.48-1984. ⊚

Library of Congress Cataloging-in-Publication Data
Liberty and hard cases / edited by Tibor R. Machan.
     p.   cm. — (Philosophic reflections on a free society)
(Hoover Institution Press publication ; no. 492)
  Includes bibliographical references (p.) and index.
  ISBN 0-8179-2802-2 (alk. paper)
    1. Disaster relief—Government policy—United States.
  2. Emergency management—Government policy—United
States.   3. Liberty.   I. Machan, Tibor R.   II. Series.
III. Hoover Institution Press publication ; 492.
HV555.U6 L5   2002
363.34′8′0973—dc21   2001039756

CONTENTS

ACKNOWLEDGMENTS

ONCE AGAIN I wish to express my gratitude to the Hoover Institution on War, Revolution and Peace, and its director, John Raisian, for supporting the publication of this work. Joanne and Johan Blokker have again given their generous support of the Hoover Institution Press series, Philosophic Reflections on a Free Society, for which I wish to express my deep gratitude. The contributing authors gave their full cooperation, patience, and conscientiousness throughout the entire publishing process. David M. Brown has helped with some editing, and I wish to thank him for this. The diligent work of Pat Baker, Ann Wood, and Marshall Blanchard of the Hoover Institution Press is also much appreciated.

CONTRIBUTORS

JOHN AHRENS is associate professor of philosophy and senior editor of the Center for Free Inquiry at Hanover College. His research is primarily in the history of political theory, with particular attention to the Roman philosophers.

N. SCOTT ARNOLD is professor of philosophy at the University of Alabama at Birmingham. He has been a visiting scholar at the Hoover Institution at Stanford University and is the author of *Marx's Radical Critique of Capitalist Society* (Oxford University Press, 1990) and *The Philosophy and Economics of Market Socialism* (Oxford University Press, 1994)

TIBOR R. MACHAN is Distinguished Fellow and Freedom Communications Professor of Business Ethics and Free Enterprise at the Leatherby Center for Entrepreneurship and Business Ethics, Argyros School of Business and Economics, Chapman University, and a Research Fellow at the Hoover Institution.

BARUN S. MITRA is a founder and presently the managing trustee of Liberty Institute, an independent public policy research and educational organization based in New Delhi, India. He has written extensively on political economic issues on the Indian subcontinent and in a wide range of publications including the *Wall Street Journal*.

AEON J. SKOBLE is assistant professor of philosophy at Bridgewater State College, in Massachusetts. He is the editor of the annual journal *Reason Papers*, and coeditor of the anthology *Political Philosophy: Essential Selections* (Prentice-Hall, 1999). His main areas of scholarship are ethics, political philosophy, and logic.

Liberty
and
Hard Cases

Tibor R. Machan

WHAT IF A tornado hits? What if a lot of tornadoes hit?

The issue in this volume isn't complicated, but it is challenging. The free society is supposed to be governed with an eye to securing the rights to life, liberty, and the pursuit of happiness. In an earlier volume of this series, *Individual Rights Reconsidered: Are the Truths of the U.S. Declaration of Independence Lasting?* we have discussed why in detail and offered numerous rebuttals to critics as well. So we shall not extensively revisit the basic issue. But we will address a problem faced by those who hold that this position is sound.

Briefly, though, a free society rests on the fact that human beings at all times, in all places, are first and foremost sovereign individuals with the capacity for self-rule, self-directedness. This capacity is a defining attribute of human beings, not merely specific to certain cultures, as some critics of classical liberalism would have it. An adult human being needs to and is capable of learning how to live and flourish independently. Any community worthy of being considered a human one must accommodate this fact about us. We are also social beings, but not just any kind of society will do our individuality justice. The novelty of the American political vision, however ill or well realized it has been, is an affirmation of the sovereignty of individuals and an established legal order in which this sovereignty is to be secured, protected, and maintained.

But what do we do when disaster strikes? Natural calamities—earthquakes, floods, tidal waves, hurricanes, tornadoes, typhoons, and the like—seem to warrant an expansion of governmental authority beyond what a free society would sanction. And government has indeed habitually stepped in with all sorts of measures whenever and wherever disasters have struck. Flood control measures are usually deemed to be its business. Few batted an eye even when the U.S. Army was called out to battle Hurricane Andrew in Florida. What is government for if not to come to the aid of citizens in such circumstances? Charles Dunlap argues that deploying the military for extraneous, nondefensive purposes is likely to convince military leaders and enthusiasts that they, not civilians, ought to be governing the country. (See Charles J. Dunlap Jr., "The Origins of the American Military Coup of 2012," *Parameters*, winter 1992–93, pp. 2–20.)

Even in personal affairs, using physical force can sometimes be justifiable—for example, when one needs to yank an unsuspecting person from the path of imminent deadly danger. John Stuart Mill argued that physically blocking someone from stepping onto a collapsing bridge is justified even in the context of adhering to the basic principles of individual liberty and minimal government.

Yet as Robert Higgs (in *Crisis and Leviathan*) and others have shown, it is nearly impossible to reestablish limits on government once it has acquired the legal authority to expand its powers for the sake of handling emergencies. In the law and in the making of public policy, precedent counts for a great deal; there is a slippery slope here. Once an approach is legitimized, extensions of power beyond the particular and special areas originally intended are almost inevitable. The definition of what constitutes an eligible emergency tends to broaden. Eventually, no dire need whatever can be neglected by lawmakers. What might slow or reverse such encroachment is a change of heart, some fear of going too far or the like. But once the logic of intervening in a particular special case has been established, it is difficult to offer a persuasive rationale for declining to apply the same logic to similar cases—unless the legitimacy of the original intervention itself is challenged. As a result, most "temporary powers" assumed by government remain part of its permanent repertoire.

Consider gun control legislation. The Second Amendment to the U.S. Constitution was undermined early on in our legislative history. And now, especially in the wake of tragic shootings—at schools, restaurants, post offices, amusement parks—it has become harder and harder to raise principled objections against more and more restrictions on the right of self-defense. Vocal members of the citizenry demand it, and the politicians have precedents.

Such decline and fall of political principles serves to underscore the integrity of those principles. They can't normally be violated, even a little, with impunity; minor incursions tend to snowball, especially when hallowed in law. Even so, a powerful tradition of political thinking challenges the value of such integrity. In contemporary U.S. politics and, indeed, around the world, it is often deemed to be a good thing to be "flexible." Principled politics is dismissed by many sophisticated thinkers as "mere ideology." Instead of ideology, they argue, we should embrace pragmatism.

The term *ideology* is burdened by a number of pejorative connotations, often imported into the implicit definition of the term. For example, there is Marx's claim that principled economic and political thinking can be nothing but rationalization for class interest (with his own economic and political thinking somehow granted exemption from this indictment, however). Those who defend a substantially laissez-faire, free market system—such as Adam Smith and David Ricardo—are on this view merely doing so to promote the class interest of capitalist, wealthy people served by such a system. Their principled advocacy amounts to nothing more than special pleading.

"Ideology" is also supposed to be the hobbyhorse of the simplistic thinker, inclining one to provide knee-jerk solutions to complex problems. This is the charge lodged against those who would apply political principles to judge what public officials ought to do in particular cases. Presumably, the resort to principle allows one, perhaps even encourages one, to ignore details of the specific context at hand.

An objective definition of ideology (i.e., one that doesn't import various charges against believers in a *particular* ideology) might be *a set of political values and doctrines advanced in support of a particular social-political system.* The definition says nothing about what those values and doctrines might be or whether their justification of a particular social system is successful. That has to be evaluated independently (i.e., the sheer fact of possessing a belief cannot be taken as proof of the falsehood or disingenuousness of that belief; it may well be that even if a capitalist says 2 plus 2 is 4, it really is 4.) And, to be sure, even the critics of ideology have ideologies of their own. Of course, theirs is usually construed as being the result of long and hard thinking and observations about community life, productive of sound judgments and evaluations; it's the other person with the other ideology who is the thoughtless propagandist for rigid and unworkable answers.

We don't have to chose between facts of the case and principles that govern, however. Politics, in fact, requires both principled thinking and proper flexibility in applying those principles to the relevant context.

Just as in our personal lives, so in politics and law we need basic ideas that serve as the foundation for understanding how human communities ought to function. And we need to practice and abide by those ideas. If they're valid, we ought not ignore them when the tough cases come along, sacrificing the long-term benefits of principled action for the sake of short-term convenience. Yet it is also vital that cases be considered in light of the detailed facts, many of which may be new and might even require some modification of the principles that guide legal decision making. New ways of communicating, new religious movements, and new forms of artistic expression all require the application of familiar principles (such as those embodied in the First Amendment) in imaginative yet consistent ways.

Certainly, it is unrealistic to expect that either flexible case-by-case assessment alone, or rigid and unreflective application of principles alone, could be sufficient to formulate sound public policy. The dogmatic approach is largely eschewed by prominent contemporary political intellectuals. However, many do regard every problem as unique, thus fostering public policies and legal decisions that do not in practice conform to any basic principles (except perhaps the principle of pragmatism itself).

As a result, those who administer public policy and law more and more have become the ultimate arbiters of what will be acceptable public policy. And that, in turn, defeats the ideal of the *rule of law*, the only reasonable alternative to the *rule of arbitrary human will*, whether of a majority, a king, or a single ruling party. The rule of law allows everyone to participate in the assessment of public policy and legal decision making; we can all evaluate whether our policy and lawmakers are doing the right thing by reference to a knowable, objective standard. If no principles apply, then anything goes. Usually, the most emotionally appealing choice of the moment is accepted, which means that those who are most adept at expressing and manipulating emotions—the demagogues—are the ones who tend to carry the day. In emergencies, especially massive emergencies that have a wide impact on a society, the opportunities for such demagoguery abound.

Is the championing of flexibility a good idea? Is it a valid approach to politics and law making? A hint that it might not be is the fact that even pragmatists may recoil from their own approach when they think the values at stake are too important to be forsaken even a little. No self-respecting moral theorist would propose that when a man forces a woman to have sex with him, the moral and legal status of the act should be mulled anew with each case. Instead everyone accepts the principle that a person has the right to choose with whom he or she will have sex and thus that any clear violation of this right is grounds for sanction. But this is the opposite of being pragmatically flexible without regard for principle.

Imagine how members of a jury in a rape case might deliberate if they were eager to be flexible and avoid being "rigid." They would steer clear of blind obedience to "dogmatic" principles—such as the need to respect the rights of the victim or to be objective about the evidence for the guilt of the defendant. Rather, the jurors would attend to such emotionally resonant considerations as whether the perpetrator is a nice person, has appealing attributes, serves the community vigilantly, promotes economic prosperity, paints well, or throws a football well. The distress of the victim may or may not enter into such a calculation. After all, what if the victim has a checkered past, is rude to the bailiff, or just doesn't emote well on the stand? By the standard of pragmatic flexibility, basing decisions on such factors may well be unimpeachable. By contrast, a principled approach would not gainsay that it is a violation of basic human rights to rape someone or that determining the guilt of the defendant on this score is the only purpose of the proceedings.

Is being principled "mere ideology"? Is it "simplistic"? Is it deficient in appropriate flexibility? No. Nor would it be simplistically ideological and excessively rigid to judge various other social matters by reference to certain tried and true principles, ones we have learned over many years of human experience with community life.

Thus, for example, when someone objects to government intrusion in the marketplace, regarding it as a violation of our economic freedom, this objection is grounded in arguably well-developed and well-established principled thinking about public economic policy. Similarly, to criticize restraint of trade because it violates private property rights and freedom of contract is no less based on tried and true principles—not as they apply to one's sovereignty over sexual matters but as they apply to one's sovereignty over economic matters.

If we accept the validity and force of moral principles in every case that the principles legitimately govern, there would be no basis for excusing lying, cheating, fraud, rape, murder, assault, kidnapping, and any of the other myriad ways people can damage their fellows. In politics, no less so than in ethics or morality, general principles come into play as we evaluate how people conduct themselves. It is not a matter of whether we need principles, only of which principles we in fact need.

Principles are tested by hard cases. Despite the temptation to abandon the principle of limited government when it comes to calamities, we might do well to encourage the development of institutions that meet the problems without the involvement of the government (private insurance policies are one such institution). Of course, the temptation to use government power is difficult to resist, and it is legitimate to ask whether the use of government power in such cases can ever be proper and consistent with the ideal of limited government or whether it must always generate that slippery slope.

We are not unfamiliar with the hazards of the slippery slope in our own personal lives. If a man hits his child in some alleged emergency, the very act of doing so may render him more amenable to smacking the kid under more typical circumstances. Slapping someone who is hysterical may make it easier to slap someone who is only very upset or recalcitrant or annoying or just too slow fetching the beer from the refrigerator. Similarly, a "minor" breach of trust can beget more of the same, a little white lie here and there can beget lying as a routine, and so forth. Moral habits promote a principled course of action even in cases where bending or breaking the principle might not seem too harmful to other parties or to our own integrity. On the other hand, granting ourselves "reasonable" exceptions tends to weaken our moral habits; as we seek to rationalize past action, differences of kind tend to devolve into differences of degree. Each new exception provides the precedent for the next, until we lose our principles altogether and doing what is right becomes a matter of happenstance and mood rather than of loyalty to enduring values.

The same is true of public action. When citizens of a country delegate to government, by means of democratic and judicial processes, the power to forge paternalistic public policies such as banning drug abuse, imposing censorship, restraining undesirable trade, and supporting desirable trade, the bureaucratic and police actions increasingly rely on the kind of violence and intrusiveness that no free citizenry ought to experience or foster. And the bureaucrats and the police tell themselves, no doubt, that what they're doing is perfectly just and right.

Consider, for starters, that when no one complains about a crime—because it is not perpetrated *against* someone but rather involves breaking a paternalistic law—to even detect the "crime" requires methods that are usually invasive. Instead of charges being brought by wronged parties, phone tapping, snooping, anonymous reporting, and undercover work are among the dubious means that lead to prosecution. Thus the role of the police shifts from protection and peacekeeping to supervision, regimentation, and reprimand. No wonder, then, that officers of the law are often caught brutalizing suspects instead of merely apprehending them. Under a paternalistic regime, their goals have multiplied, and thus the means they see as necessary to achieving those goals multiply too.

The same general danger of corrupting a free society's system of laws may arise when government is called on to deal with calamities. There is the perception, of course, that in such circumstances the superior powers of government are indispensable, given the immediateness of the danger. The immediate benefits—a life saved by a marine—are evident. Yet the dangers of extensive involvement by legal authorities in the handling of nonjudicial problems are no less evident, if less immediate in impact.

The contributors to this work set out to explore (a) whether government action is indispensable under such circumstances and (b) what might be done to restrain the expansion of the scope of governmental power if indeed emergency circumstances warrant governmental intervention.

This is a work in normative political theory and public policy. Contributors are at times examining imaginary cases, doing thought experiments, with the aid of what might be considered approximations of historical models.

This approach is typical not only in scholarship and research on normative human affairs (where experimentation is precluded unless conducted on volunteers) but also in ordinary life. We often wonder how we might best acquit ourselves under difficult circumstances, even if we realize that rarely does everyone do his or her best at the task. The point is, we might do our best if we prepare well. Asking "what if?" helps us prepare.

So what if a fully free society were battered by calamities? Could it preserve its liberty while also handling the emergencies promptly and well? This is the question taken up by contributors to the present volume.

CHAPTER ONE

The Role of Government in Responding to Natural Catastrophes

N. Scott Arnold

GOVERNMENT AND THE CATASTROPHE INSURANCE MARKET

Natural disasters are a permanent feature of the human condition. Hurricanes, floods, earthquakes, and tornadoes are the most high-profile types of natural disasters that occur in the United States. The first three of these cause special problems because of the large number of people they affect and the way losses are distributed. As a society's population grows and becomes wealthier, their impact becomes greater, at least by some measures. Although deaths and injuries associated with hurricanes, floods, and earthquakes in the United States have declined, the number of people affected has increased. Annual population growth rates in Florida and California, the two states that are most subject to hurricanes and earthquakes, respectively have been two to three times the national average for decades. During 1970–90 the population of Southeast Atlantic coastal counties—prime targets for hurricanes—increased by 75 percent, four times the national average. When one considers the rising financial costs of natural disasters, the figures are alarming.

Real dollar damages of a given-sized natural disaster have been doubling every fourteen years. In the period 1992–97, eleven catastrophes have cost more than $1 billion each. The two mega-catastrophes of recent years, Hurricane Andrew in 1992 and the Northridge earthquake in 1994, cost $18 billion and $23 billion, respectively. The federal government's share of the costs of these two events—$28 billion—is more than its combined spending on higher education, pollution control, and running the federal court system.[1]

Private insurance has traditionally handled most of the costs associated with property loss consequent to natural catastrophes, and it still does for more localized disasters such as tornadoes. The private sector absorbed 81 percent of the costs associated with Hurricane Andrew and 55 percent of the costs associated with the Northridge earthquake. However, insurance companies have become increasingly skittish; they paid out $12.5 billion for the Northridge quake, which works out to $1,352 per person for those living in Los Angeles County. This payout equaled the entire amount of premiums collected in this century for earthquake insurance. In Florida, Hurricane Andrew caused insured losses of $15.5 billion; this was 50 percent more than all premiums collected in Florida for the past twenty-two years. Insurers have additional reasons to worry about Florida: the state adds about 130,000 households each year, the coastal population has grown 37 percent (from 7.7 million to 10.5 million) from 1980 to 1993, and three-fourths of the state's population now resides in coastal counties. Property at risk will soon reach $1 trillion, and estimates are that a major hurricane making landfall around Miami could inflict $51 billion in damages.[2]

---

1. On the growing costs of natural disasters, see Kenneth A. Froot, *The Financing of Catastrophic Risk* (Chicago: University of Chicago Press, 1999), pp. 1–22; and Bill Emerson and Ted Stevens, "Natural Disasters: A Budget Time Bomb," *Washington Post*, October 31, 1995, p. A13.

2. The figures about earthquakes come from Richard J. Ross Sr., "Earth-

The insurance situation in both California and Florida has been significantly complicated by state government intervention. In 1985, the state government in California passed a law requiring insurance companies to offer earthquake insurance as an optional rider on all homeowners' policies. Homeowners did not have to buy the insurance, but companies had to offer it. Ironically, the industry itself initially wanted this requirement because a lower court decision seemed to indicate it would be liable for earthquake damage on standard homeowners' policies, even though policy-holders had not purchased an earthquake endorsement and companies had received no premiums to cover that damage. The decision was later overturned, but the law stayed on the books. Companies did not aggressively market earthquake insurance, however, and few enough policies were written so that the industry felt comfortable with their exposure. Everything changed after the Northridge quake. Payments in the Northridge area itself averaged $30,000 to $40,000 per claim after the 10 percent deductible. In light of these payouts and the enormous and unanticipated destruction wrought by the quake, earthquake insurance suddenly became very desirable for property owners. However, the same facts gave insurance companies cause to worry about their exposure and the consequent risk of insolvency. In light of this, they did not want to write any more of this insurance. Given the legal requirement to offer earthquake insurance, which the government of California was not about to change, the only alternative to leaving the state

---

quake Insurance Protection in California," in Howard Kunreuther and Richard J. Ross Sr., *Paying the Price* (Washington, D.C.: National Academy of Sciences, Joseph Henry Press, 1998), pp. 67–95. The figures on hurricanes come from David A. Moss, "Courting Disaster? The Transformation of Federal Disaster Policy Since 1803," in Froot, *Financing Catastrophic Risk*, pp. 307–51; and from Eugen LeComte and Karen Gahagan, "Hurricane Insurance Protection in Florida," in Kunreuther and Ross, *Paying the Price*, pp. 97–124. The cited works by Ross and by LeComte and Gahagan also contain good discussions of the insurance situation in California and Florida, respectively.

for most companies was to continue to renew existing policies but to stop writing new homeowners' policies. About 90 percent of companies doing business in California did this or imposed significant restrictions on their intake of new business. It is obvious that the inability to get homeowners' insurance when purchasing a home would wreak havoc with real estate markets, so something had to be done.

As is usually the case when government intervention disrupts the market for a good or service, the cure for the resultant problems is more government intervention. In 1996, in response to this crisis, the state created the California Earthquake Authority (CEA), a state-run insurance company. It sold earthquake insurance policies in the residential market through private insurance companies. The deductible was set at a very high level, 15 percent. This effectively meant that a house had to be located within twenty miles of a fault or on very unstable soil to sustain damage that would exceed the deductible. Rates varied from $3 to $7 per $1,000 of coverage. Given the explosive growth in real estate values in high-risk areas of California, it is evident that many homeowners were facing premiums of a thousand dollars a year and up.

Not surprisingly, Californians have been reluctant to buy or renew earthquake insurance, and the CEA is writing about half the policies it expected to write. In some areas, the number of policies in effect is declining precipitously as nonrenewals outpace the writing of new policies. Nor have private insurers been eager to sell them, in part because of the complex funding mechanism for the CEA. In the event of a quake, private insurers would be liable for a percentage (which matches their share of the market) of the first $720 million in losses. In addition, they are collectively subject to a postquake assessment on the order of $2.16 billion, which is also proportioned according to market share. The basic problem facing the industry—how to limit their exposure and the consequent risk of insolvency—has not been adequately addressed.

In the aftermath of Hurricane Andrew, insurance companies in Florida faced similar problems and difficulties. The hurricane itself caused insured losses of $15.5 billion. Insurers then learned that it would be very expensive to get reinsurance on the various lines they offer, including, most notably, homeowners' insurance. (Reinsurance policies insure insurance companies against losses in excess of a given amount.) Also, new information from catastrophic risk models indicated that their exposure might be much greater than anticipated. Finally, they worried about hidden exposures that are tied to mandated residual market mechanisms, such as guaranty funds. A guaranty fund is responsible for claims against companies that become insolvent. For example, after Andrew, the Florida Insurance Guaranty Fund (FIGA) was activated to cover claims against nine insurance companies, which became insolvent as a result of that catastrophe. Payments totaled $400 million. The fund had to borrow the money by issuing bonds and then pay it back through its normal funding mechanism—legally mandated assessments on solvent insurance companies. In the aftermath of Andrew, these assessments doubled. In effect, the solvent companies had to cover the losses of the insolvent companies. In sum, in Florida as in California, insurance companies discovered they had been running imprudent risks, and thus they wanted to limit the amount of coverage they were writing.

To address these problems, the state of Florida did a number of things. First, it issued a temporary order prohibiting withdrawal from the market by insurance companies, a prohibition that was not fully rescinded until November 1999. It then created the Florida Hurricane Catastrophe Fund, a kind of reinsurance fund that enabled companies to renew policies they would have otherwise canceled. The state also established the Joint Underwriting Association (JUA), which serves as the "insurer of last resort" for those whose policies were canceled or not renewed. As of June 30, 1996, the JUA held more than 910,000 policies, making it the second-largest insurer in the state. Funding for these residual market mechanisms has come from mandatory assessments on insurance companies. All of them (FIGA, FHCF, JUA) are ways of forcing insurance companies to bear, or to contribute to bearing, risks they would otherwise shun.

The other substantial role that the government—this time the federal government—has in the catastrophe insurance market is through the National Flood Insurance Program (NFIP), which was started in 1968.[3] Catastrophic floods have been a recurring phenomenon in many parts of the country, most notably the Midwest, but also in areas prone to hurricanes; much of the damage to property that hurricanes inflict is through flooding from the associated heavy rains, and most homeowners' policies do not cover flooding (though they do cover wind damage and wind-induced water damage). Historically, private insurers had been unable to offer affordable flood insurance and make a profit, in part because of their inability to develop a rate structure that accurately reflected the risks involved. NFIP addressed this problem. Central to this program has been the development of Flood Insurance Rate Maps (FIRMs) for communities that are at risk for flooding. The FIRMs include a detailed assessment of risks within a given community and floodplain and provide a basis for land-use regulations and building codes that mitigate damages, should a flood occur. The study to develop the FIRMs was a massive effort, costing $1.154 billion through 1997, and it has produced a wealth of information about the risks property owners face and advice about what might be done to mitigate them.

Crucial to the success of NFIP's insurance program was participation by at-risk communities and support from the home mort-

---

3. For information on NFIP, see Edward T. Pasterick, "The National Flood Insurance Program," in Kunreuther and Ross, *Paying the Price*, pp. 125–54; and Moss, "Courting Disaster?" in Froot, *Financing Catastrophic Risk*, pp. 307–51.

gage industry. The federal government assumed local communities would be eager to participate and that flood insurance would be treated like casualty insurance by lenders, that is, lenders would require it as a condition of a home loan. The disaster of Hurricane Agnes in 1972 revealed, however, that both assumptions were incorrect. Community participation in NFIP was low, and few homeowners had flood insurance. In 1973, Congress required flood insurance for federally backed mortgages and made participation in NFIP a prerequisite for eligibility for disaster relief. Despite these efforts, lenders were not vigilant in forcing people to renew flood insurance every year and private lenders were not requiring it, so in 1994 measures were enacted to get more people into the program, including giving lenders the option of "forceplacing" insurance on recalcitrant property owners.

A key feature of NFIP is the rate structure for the premiums that property owners pay. There are two types of rates: (1) actuarial rates, which apply to structures outside the 100-year floodplain and to new or retrofitted structures inside the plain that are in compliance with the FIRM, and (2) "subsidized" rates, which apply to structures inside the floodplain built before the FIRM was conducted. The "subsidy" does not represent a direct infusion of cash to supplement premiums but instead consists of charging property owners lower, nonactuarial premiums; this practice, which was originally designed to maximize participation in NFIP's insurance program, has prevented NFIP from accumulating reserves to cover heavy losses in years when there is a lot of flooding. Over the years, there has been an ongoing, though not entirely successful, attempt to phase out subsidies by raising premiums. In 1978, about 75 percent of policies were subsidized; by 1997 only about 35 percent were subsidized. However, in this latter group, people pay only about 38 percent of the actuarial rate. This is a substantial subsidy, both relatively and absolutely. Moreover, NFIP has operated under a rule that allows repeated payment on policies for damages less than 50 percent of the value of the structure. This has allowed people to rebuild repeatedly in flood-prone areas. In other words, a property owner could suffer 49 percent damage to a structure, rebuild, get hit by another flood, suffer 49 percent damages, rebuild again, and so on. These "grandfathered" structures have been responsible for somewhere between one-third and one-half of the total claims dollars paid out over the years. Moreover, the "subsidy" now costs about half a billion a year in forgone premiums. Because of these artificially low premiums, NFIP experienced cumulative operating losses from 1969 to 1980 of $817,680,000. The total amount borrowed from the Treasury prior to 1986 was $1.2 billion, which was repaid not with higher premiums but with congressional appropriations. From 1993 to 1997, the program experienced $3.4 billion in losses and had to borrow almost $1 billion. Currently, there are about four million NFIP policies in force, but, by some estimates, this represents only about half the number of policies that should be held.

There is one final form of catastrophe insurance that merits brief mention. The federal government offers subsidized multiperil crop insurance to farmers, and one of those perils is flood. Premiums are heavily subsidized. From 1977 to 1993, losses plus administrative expenses (which is the net cost to taxpayers) have averaged $588 million more than what was collected in premiums.[4] Despite the subsidies, participation rates have remained relatively low, which has led to more direct bailouts when disasters strike.

DIRECT DISASTER ASSISTANCE

When one turns from insurance to more direct disaster assistance, government involvement is also substantial and has increased

---

4. For further discussion of crop insurance, see Moss, "Courting Disaster?" in Froot, *Financing Catastrophic Risk*, pp. 320–22.

throughout the twentieth century, especially at the federal level.[5] To get a sense of that growth, it is instructive to compare the federal response to the great Mississippi flood in 1927 with the response to the flood of the same river in 1993. In 1927 federal assistance was limited to lending equipment and personnel (often military) to relief efforts. Total expenditures amounted to about $10 million, which was about 3.3 percent of total damages. The American Red Cross, by comparison, collected about $23.5 million in donations and provided emergency services to about 600,000 residents over a fourteen-month period. The Red Cross, together with governmental agencies at all levels, covered only about 13 percent of the total damages. By contrast, in 1993 President Bill Clinton declared all of Iowa and many counties in other states disaster areas, making them eligible for various forms of federal relief. Numerous federal agencies got involved, spearheaded by FEMA (Federal Emergency Management Agency), and a supplemental appropriations bill was passed. Although the bill started at $2.5 billion, the final package reached $6.3 billion, about half the total estimated damage. As federal commitments to disaster relief grew, private commitments were attenuated. In 1953, the Red Cross outspent the federal government on natural disasters by a ratio of 1.6 to 1.0. By 1966, the latter outspent the Red Cross by a ratio of 8 to 1.

The Mississippi flood of 1993 was not the most expensive disas-

5. For an overview of the history of disaster relief in the United States, see Moss, "Courting Disaster?" in Froot, *Financing Catastrophic Risk*, pp. 307–51. For current government policy, see Moss, ibid.; Christopher M. Lewis and Kevin C. Murdock, "Alternative Means of Redistributing Catastrophic Risk in a National Risk Management System," in Froot, *Financing Catastrophic Risk*, pp. 51–85; and Howard Kunreuther, "Introduction," in Kunreuther and Ross, *Paying the Price*, pp. 1–15. Subsidies to farmers are discussed in George L. Priest, "The Government, the Market, and the Problem of Catastrophic Loss," *Journal of Risk and Uncertainty* 1996, 12:219–37. Details about programs run by FEMA and the SBA can be downloaded from their websites at http://www.fema.gov/r-n-r/ and http://www.sba.gov/disaster/, respectively. Facts and figures on direct assistance in this and subsequent paragraphs are drawn from all these sources.

ter for the federal government. That honor goes to the Northridge earthquake. Governmental outlays (mostly federal) on that disaster have been estimated at about $10 billion.

This is about as much as the government spent in one year on its main social welfare program (AFDC) at the time. Hurricane Andrew, which hit the year before the Mississippi flood, cost the government about $3.42 billion. In addition to regular appropriations for agencies such as FEMA, there have been six major supplemental appropriations for natural disasters since 1988, totaling $17 billion. Also, disaster declarations are made not just for large-scale catastrophes such as earthquakes, hurricanes, and major floods but for other adverse events such as tornadoes, forest fires, winter freezes, snowstorms, and severe summer storms. In 1999, forty-nine major disaster declarations were issued.

Direct aid subsequent to disaster declaration takes various forms; there are of course the expenses associated with rescuing people and dealing with the immediate aftermath of a disaster (enforcement of curfews, provision of temporary shelter, etc.). This includes the activities of police, emergency response personnel, and, on occasion, the military. The National Guard enforces curfews and prevents looting; the military also has heavy equipment that can be used to move debris, reopen roads, and so on. These forms of direct aid represent a relatively small part of the federal government's costs of disaster relief, however. More consequential are the costs associated with the repair of government facilities. Under the Stafford Disaster Relief and Assistance Act of 1988, at least 75 percent of the costs of repairing state and local government facilities is borne by the federal government. Supplemental appropriations for Hurricane Andrew, the 1993 Mississippi floods, and the 1994 Northridge quake covered up to 100 percent of these costs—despite the fact that private insurance is often available to cover these losses.

Other disaster-related spending includes direct grants and loans. The Small Business Administration (SBA) provides disaster loans for businesses that cover uninsured losses up to $1.5 million. Loan rates are subsidized, depending on whether or not other credit is available; if other credit is available, rates range from 7.25 percent to 7.5 percent. If no other credit is available, the rate is 3.63 percent. The SBA also offers subsidized loans of up to $200,000 for uninsured losses to property and up to $40,000 for uninsured losses of personal property. Individuals (homeowners and renters) not eligible for SBA loans can get direct grants from FEMA in amounts up to $13,900. FEMA will also pay up to eighteen months' rent or mortgage payments, and provides small grants for home repairs. Finally, grants are also often made to farmers through special appropriations, whether or not they have signed up for crop insurance; payments are slightly more generous to those who took out crop insurance.

The level of these payments is determined by applying a complex formula on a county-by-county basis. The application of the formula is done by local boards, on which sit some of the insured, their friends, and neighbors. Not surprisingly, inflated claims have been submitted to these boards by farmers whose crops have been inundated.

The preceding discussion gives some sense of the nature and level of government involvement in dealing with the consequences of natural disasters. To summarize, that involvement consists of the following activities, which can be usefully categorized under the headings of insurance and direct aid:

Insurance

1. *Earthquake insurance in California.* The government of California requires private companies doing business in California to offer quake insurance and to contribute to the funding of the California Earthquake Authority (CEA), which underwrites these policies.

2. *Homeowners' insurance in Florida.* The government of Florida has required private companies to continue writing homeowners' policies in the state and to participate in various residual market mechanisms as a way of making hurricane coverage available.

3. *Flood insurance.* The federal government offers flood insurance through the National Flood Insurance Program (NFIP). Property owners with existing structures inside the floodplain are charged nonactuarial rates, which creates an implicit subsidy.

4. *Crop insurance.* The federal government offers farmers subsidized crop insurance, which can be triggered by natural disasters such as flooding.

Direct Aid

1. Emergency aid from government agencies and government employees at the time of the disaster and immediately following it

2. Federal funding to repair state and local government facilities

3. Loans and grants from the Small Business Administration

4. Grants to individuals from FEMA and occasional assistance to flooded-out farmers whether nor not they purchased crop insurance

EVALUATING THE ROLE OF GOVERNMENT

Some of this government involvement in dealing with natural disasters is clearly difficult to defend. Not only is the crop insurance program subject to conflicts of interest and self-dealing that borders on fraud, but the government undercuts its own program by occasionally offering another policy in which insurance is provided for free! This is what happens when special appropriations bills include payments to farmers without crop insurance.

Federal government indemnification of state and local governments for damages to public facilities is almost as difficult to defend. Studies indicate that local governments have shown little interest in mitigation measures (i.e, measures that reduce the probability and/ or severity of loss), nor have they purchased insurance against catastrophes, even though such insurance is available from the private sector.[6] This is almost certainly not coincidental. It is not in the interests of smaller governmental units to spend scarce resources on mitigation and insurance if the federal government is going to offer an insurance policy that provides 75 percent coverage with a 25 percent copay at absolutely no cost in premiums. The obvious justification for bailing out victims of disaster—they couldn't afford to take precautions or bear the costs of repair and restoration in the event of an adverse event—is hardly applicable to governmental units that have taxing authority and can issue tax-free bonds to fund repairs after the fact.

Is there any role for government in disaster relief? Few would object to the kind of immediate aid provided by police and emergency personnel during and immediately after a natural disaster. Law enforcement, evacuation, search and rescue, repair and maintenance of roads, bridges, and other infrastructure are all traditional government activities that cannot be easily handled through the private sector.

As indicated, however, it is difficult to justify federal responsibility for repairing state and local infrastructure. Other forms of direct aid appear to be easier to justify, at least to the extent that they go to the least advantaged. Special disaster unemployment insurance

6. See Raymond Burby, *Sharing Environmental Risks* (Boulder, Colo.: Westview Press, 1992); and Steven French and Gary Rudholm, "Damage to Public Property in the Whittier Narrows Earthquake: Implications for Earthquake Insurance," *Earthquake Spectra* 1990, 6:105–23.

payments, small grants to lower-income homeowners and renters, and subsidized loans might be supported on the grounds that these individuals simply could not afford insurance and/or mitigation measures. Besides, it would be politically impossible to tell these people they are completely on their own following a natural disaster. In the case of people who are better off, however, assistance beyond that which meets emergency needs in the immediate aftermath of a disaster is more problematic. Lending uninsured businesses up to $1.5 million, lending uninsured (nonpoor) individuals money at below-market rates, and outright grants to the nonpoor are difficult to defend in light of the availability of private insurance to cover these losses. It also creates a moral hazard problem; to the extent that people believe the government will bail them out in the case of a natural disaster, they are less likely to purchase insurance and to take mitigation measures that will limit their losses in the event of a disaster.

What about catastrophe insurance? Insurance against hurricanes, floods, and earthquakes presents special problems for the private sector that are thought to justify government provision of this form of insurance. In what follows I explain and critically evaluate the case for government-provided insurance of the sort provided by NFIP. I then critically appraise the regulatory regimes for earthquake insurance in California and homeowners' insurance in Florida as alternative solutions to the special problems that have arisen in these two states.

In the 1890s and again in the mid-1920s, the insurance industry wrote flood insurance policies but sustained such large losses that it withdrew from the market. As flood insurance was being discussed in government circles in the 1950s and 1960s, the private sector indicated that it would not get involved in a major way, which in part explains why the government did. One of the problems for private insurance companies in this connection is that the risks associated with floods (unlike most other casualties) are *correlated risks*, meaning that the probability that one policyholder will suffer an adverse event is not independent of the probability that another policyholder will suffer a like adverse event. In the context of flood insurance, this means that if one policyholder is flooded out, it is much more likely that other policyholders will be flooded out as well. By contrast, adverse events for which people buy other kinds of casualty insurance, such as auto accidents, are uncorrelated. If I have a motor vehicle accident, that does not affect the probability that others who have policies with my company will also have an auto accident.

The problem with correlated risks for private insurance companies is *not* that their expected loss is greater for correlated risks than for uncorrelated risks.[7] Rather, the problem is that the *variance* is higher for correlated risks. Roughly, the idea is that a company runs a greater risk of having to pay enormous aggregate claims in a given period that could render it insolvent when the risks they insure against are correlated than when risks are uncorrelated. In the case of uncorrelated risks, the law of large numbers implies that the chances are good that the total claims made for any given period (e.g., a year) will be closer to the expected losses. By contrast, natural catastrophes, which occur more rarely, are not as likely to produce a stable claims experience. Insurance companies are more subject to feast (no disasters) or famine (one or more large disasters) in the case of correlated risks. Since companies worry about their solvency, they are more reluctant to write policies on correlated risks, and the risks associated with floods (as well as hurricanes and earthquakes) are highly correlated. Since governments cannot go broke as easily, they are better able to handle correlated risks asso-

---

7. The expected loss for a set of policyholders is determined by multiplying the probability of an adverse event times the maximum payout a company would have to make. Whether risks are correlated or uncorrelated, the expected loss is the same, assuming that the probability of an adverse event is the same and the level of coverage is the same.

ciated with natural disasters. In addition, private insurance companies must pay taxes on earnings from investments that constitute their reserves. Governments have an advantage in this regard, since they do not face those tax liabilities.

A second major difficulty facing the private sector in writing flood insurance is the adverse selection problem. Essentially, adverse selection occurs when low-risk policyholders must subsidize high-risk policyholders because the insureds know more about their individual risks than the insurers do. Under these circumstances, if insurers charge all policyholders the same premiums, the high-risk policyholders would flock to the policy because they would be subsidized by the low-risk policyholders; assuming the low risks also have a more accurate estimate of their true risks than insurers do, they will cancel their policies or not insure in the first place. The insurer will be left with only the high-risk policyholders. The insurer will either exit the market for that form of insurance or charge everyone a premium appropriate to the high-risk policyholders. In either case, mutually beneficial trades will be forgone as the low-risk property owners are unable to get coverage at a mutually beneficial price (i.e., an actuarially fair rate). This is a classic case of market failure (which for some is almost a sufficient condition for government involvement). Of course, insurers can always gather more information in an effort to identify the high-risk and low-risk policyholders so that they can be charged different premiums, but gathering this information is usually costly and may drive premium prices to prohibitive levels. The adverse selection problem was one reason insurance companies withdrew from the flood insurance market in the 1920s.

How can the government solve this problem? For flood insurance, it was solved by producing the FIRMs (Flood Insurance Rate Maps) at taxpayer expense. Among other things, the FIRMs provide accurate and valuable information about the contours of the hundred-year floodplain[8] and the associated risks. The government used that information to develop actuarially fair rates for new and rebuilt structures within that floodplain. The decision to charge less than actuarially fair rates to owners of existing structures (a policy that is supposed to be phased out over time) was a deliberate decision whose rationale was to maximize participation in the program at the outset. Firms offering a new and unfamiliar product often adopt a below-cost pricing strategy at the beginning of a marketing campaign to build product awareness. It has also been suggested that it would be unfair to charge full, actuarially fair rates at the outset to property owners who did not previously know they were at high risk of being flooded out. Ultimately, however, the government seeks an actuarially sound system in which subsidies have been eliminated.

As NFIP moves in this direction, it also solves, at least in part, another problem that faces the insurance industry—the moral hazard problem, which occurs when possession of insurance induces behavior that makes it more likely that a claim (or a more expensive claim) will be filed. In the case of flood insurance, the morally hazardous behavior consists in failing to adopt mitigation measures (including not building in parts of the floodplain) that reduce the likelihood of a claim or the damage a flood would cause to an insured structure. Although moral hazard problems associated with "grandfathered" structures have plagued NFIP from its inception, new and rebuilt structures must be built in accordance with new building codes, which make these structures more flood resistant, which in turn means that the size and incidence of future claims should decline. The government is also buying out entire at-risk

---

8. This term is widely used but misleading. It does not designate an area that is flooded once every hundred years but instead designates an area that has at least a 1 percent chance of being inundated in any given year.

communities, which will further curb adverse selection and moral hazard problems.[9]

Although the case for substantial government involvement in flood insurance, and by extension other forms of catastrophe insurance, appears strong, appearances are misleading. The fundamental problem is that government involvement in catastrophe insurance forces a redistribution of risks and costs that is morally indefensible. To see why, notice that the government faces distinctive moral hazard problems of its own when it provides catastrophe insurance. Consider the National Flood Insurance Program. The fact that NFIP has never paid its own way is significant. For decades it has charged the most at-risk property owners premiums that are about one-third of the actuarially fair rate, and it has allowed stricken property owners to rebuild repeatedly in the same location as long as damage in any single flood is less than 50 percent of the assessed value. Although the private sector sometimes offers a new and unfamiliar product at below cost, it does not do so for decades, and it controls losses by canceling policies for property owners who have repeated large claims. NFIP has continued to charge some policyholders as little as one-third of the full, actuarially fair rate, but it has not gone out of business in years when massive floods struck (including the 1993 flooding of the Mississippi River). What prevented this was its borrowing authority, backed by the U.S. Congress. When NFIP had to borrow money to pay claims, it retired the debt not through assessments on policyholders but by appropriations from Congress. This meant that taxpayers had to foot some of the bill after the fact, which meant that some property owners have been subsidized by everyone else who pays taxes. Since a government insurance company faces virtually no prospect of

9. However, this buyout program creates a significant moral hazard problem of its own. If property owners believe the government will buy them out after the next major flood, they have a reduced incentive to take out insurance to cover those losses.

bankruptcy, its directors have less incentive to charge actuarially fair rates; indeed, in the case of NFIP, its directors have had a positive incentive to undercharge some of its policyholders, since by so doing it could further another of the program's goals—increased participation in NFIP.

The redistribution of resources from taxpayers to policyholders is particularly insidious in the case of NFIP because the premium subsidy is not paid in an above-board appropriation on a year-by-year basis; instead, it is done in the manner just indicated: NFIP simply undercharges some policyholders, borrows when huge claims must be paid, and then goes to Congress for a bailout when it cannot pay its debts.

Forced redistribution operates in more subtle and even less defensible ways in the homeowners' insurance market in Florida and the earthquake insurance market in California. State governments have erected exit barriers by prohibiting insurance companies from canceling or not writing new policies in Florida or, in the case of California, by forcing companies to offer quake insurance to all homeowners. Companies are faced with the prospect of leaving the state entirely or accepting greater risks than they otherwise would take. The former option means forgoing business in ordinary casualty and other insurance lines (e.g., auto, life, and health insurance). Some of the potential catastrophic losses facing these companies can be offset by charging higher premiums for these other lines of insurance, though there are obvious limits to how much of this sort of thing they can do before they lose business to out-of-state competitors who do not face this mandate because they do not write homeowners' insurance. The affected companies can also raise rates for in-state homeowners who do not face high risks of hurricane or quake damage. Stockholders (or out-of-state policyholders in mutual insurance companies) are also forced to subsidize at-risk homeowners to the extent that this sort of state action lowers share prices or reduces dividends. Finally, state taxpayers generally are on the hook, to the extent that tax dollars are used to capitalize residual market mechanisms, such as Florida's JUA, which serves as an "insurer of last resort."

Is there any way to justify these various forms of coercive redistribution? One might conceive of the redistribution involved in government-provided insurance (as well as direct government assistance) as part of the normal workings of a multiperil insurance policy that all persons living in the country in question have. The redistribution is a natural consequence of risk spreading, which has been made fairer or more insurance-like in recent years by the expanding role of FEMA in dealing with other natural disasters, such as tornadoes, droughts, forest fires, and snowstorms. The problem with this rationale is that it lumps together heterogeneous risks in ways that people would never voluntarily agree to. Many citizens face almost no risk of the most devastating catastrophes (earthquakes, tornadoes, hurricanes, and flooding), and others face some of these risks but not others. If disaster relief and insurance subsidies were to be treated as part of national catastrophe insurance policy, the government would make at least some effort to collect differential premiums for different levels of risk.[10] Not only is much of the funding out of general revenues paid for by taxpayers who face little risk of natural catastrophes, but some of it (especially in California and Florida) is surreptitiously imposed nationwide on policyholders and stockholders of insurance companies through various regulatory burdens. The pattern of benefits and burdens in no way approximates an insurance scheme.

Another possible justification for the coercive redistribution involved in catastrophe insurance begins with a general principle of the welfare state that the costs of misfortunes beyond people's con-

10. As Richard Epstein has pointed out, "within the political system, the equilibrium position tends to be one that moves toward equal insurance rates for all customers, *regardless* of insurable risk." Epstein, "Catastrophic Response to Catastrophic Risk," *Journal of Risk and Uncertainty* 1996, 12:287–308.

trol should be socialized by the state. To put it in other terms, it is unfair to force citizens who are subject to unchosen risks to bear the full costs of those risks. If the risks associated with natural disasters that property owners face are unchosen or involuntary, then it is appropriate to socialize their losses, at least to some extent.

Whether or not this general principle about unchosen risks is defensible, a little reflection makes it clear that it is simply inapplicable in the case of risks of natural catastrophes. Although no one chooses to be a victim of a natural catastrophe, people routinely choose to put themselves at risk for one. For many decades, California and Florida have experienced substantial immigration from the rest of the country and, in the case of California, from the rest of the world.

It is ironic that these two states, which are most attractive for reasons of climate, natural beauty, and good economic conditions, are also the most prone to expensive natural disasters. However, that irony cannot obscure the fact that millions of people choose to live there in the knowledge of the natural disasters that threaten, and they are subsidized by people living in less agreeable climes and more economically distressed areas. Longtime residents also know—sometimes from personal experience—that they live in harm's way. Although individuals typically have no detailed knowledge of the extent of their risks, they do know that these risks exist and are nontrivial.

Similarly, it requires an expansive notion of involuntariness to conclude that most, or even many, residents of hundred-year floodplains throughout the nation have involuntarily assumed the risks of flooding. This is so for a number of reasons. First, many of the areas most at risk for flooding have experienced major floods in the not-too-distant past; historical memories of these floods are vivid and long-lasting in affected communities.

Second, in the past decade or so, the government has mapped flood zones and conducted an extensive public awareness campaign to alert the public to the fact that homeowners' insurance does not cover this risk. The private mortgage industry now routinely requires flood insurance as a condition for a home loan.[11] Given the facts, the decision of people to stay on these properties, even on multigenerational family farms, can hardly be described as the assumption of an unchosen or involuntary risk. The government should no more be subsidizing insurance for high-risk property owners than it should be subsidizing auto insurance for unmarried males under the age of twenty-five, whose risk factors, it is worth noting, are less voluntary than those of property owners who live in at-risk areas.

Although the case for government intervention in the catastrophe insurance market is weak, the above criticisms lack practical significance unless there is a feasible private alternative. Could the provision of catastrophe insurance be done entirely by the private sector? Unless a purely private alternative is feasible, it is difficult to see how a politically sustainable case could be made for getting government out of this business.

THE FEASIBILITY OF
PRIVATE CATASTROPHE INSURANCE

For a purely private-sector alternative to work, it would have to be able to solve the problems of correlated risks and adverse selection. Both of these problems can in fact be solved; let us begin with the problem of correlated risks. Although risks are often described as correlated relative to a particular adverse event or kind of adverse event (e.g., flood, earthquake), strictly speaking that is not accurate. A correlated risk is defined relative to a set of *policyholders* whose policies are held by a particular company for a specified line of

---

11. Personal communication from Laurie Trimm, a loan officer with the National Bank of Commerce, Birmingham, Alabama.

insurance. For example, it might be said that the risks associated with a tornado are highly correlated within the path of the storm, but that is not correct. If property owners in the path of a storm are insured by many different insurers, the losses are not correlated at all. More generally, the relevant comparison class for determining the correlation of risks for tornadoes is all the homeowners' policies a particular company writes that include wind damage. For national companies, the risks associated with tornadoes are spread throughout the nation. Furthermore, because of the frequency of these storms, the law of large numbers operates to keep the variance down and push aggregate claims for a given period (e.g., a year) closer to the expected loss. This is why the risks associated with tornadoes are not highly correlated for most companies.

Floods occur in virtually every state, and one would expect that in a purely private flood insurance market (e.g., if NFIP were privatized), insurance companies would limit their exposure in any area subject to major flooding. The insurance industry is not particularly concentrated, so one would expect that many companies would enter the market in any particular floodplain so that no one company had too many of its eggs in one basket. Companies would diversify their risks by writing policies in floodplains located in different parts of the country—at least if they could be assured that they would not be taken hostage by state regulators in the way they have in Florida or California. This assurance is within the power of the federal government under the Interstate Commerce clause; it could simply modify the provisions of the McCarran-Ferguson Act, which delegates insurance regulation to the states. That act has served as the excuse by state regulators to bolt the exits and to force companies to bear the risks of natural disasters they would otherwise not bear.

Purely private flood insurance assumes, of course, that insurance companies would be able to determine the risks they face, something they could not do very well in the early and mid–twentieth century. The FIRMs provided by NFIP fill this gap nicely, however. At a cost of more than $1 billion, the government has developed the information necessary for the private sector to take over this market. And, indeed, there has been movement in that direction under an NFIP program known as "Write-Your-Own" in which insurance companies participate more fully in writing flood insurance. NFIP could be entirely privatized by transferring full underwriting responsibility to private firms.

What about the risks associated with hurricanes? In the homeowners' insurance market in Florida, assuming it was unencumbered by the current regulatory regime, one would expect that firms would want to reduce their exposure in light of their experience with Hurricane Andrew by canceling homeowners' policies or excluding hurricane damage. This would create a ready market for firms that could diversify their risks by writing policies (either limited to hurricanes or broader homeowners' policies) in different parts of the Southeast (and Hawaii) that are subject to hurricanes. A problem with the risks associated with hurricanes, however, is that their numbers are rising, both because of a cyclical upswing in the occurrence and severity of hurricanes and because of increased development throughout the Southeast, especially in Florida. A private, deregulated insurance market, with higher premiums for many, no doubt, would not lessen the number of tropical storms each year, but it would send some important signals to developers and immigrants (including risk-averse retirees) to reconsider their plans and/or to pursue mitigation strategies more intensively.

Finally, what about the problem of correlated risks associated with earthquakes? Private insurers writing quake insurance need not face this problem. They are facing it now because the state has forced companies to distribute their underwriting. Before the court ruling that led the industry to favor mandatory offers of quake insurance, companies' exposure was low because few people had such a policy. This meant that insurance companies did not have to pay careful attention to the risk of earthquakes when they wrote homeowners' policies since most of their policies did not include quake damage. When the court ruling said they might have to pay on earthquake damage anyway, they pushed through a mandatory offer provision as a defensive measure. As a result, they found themselves with more highly correlated risks than they would have voluntarily accepted, though this was better than being forced to offer free quake insurance, which is what the court ruling had portended.

Geologic and engineering studies undertaken in California in recent years (some funded by the government) have made it possible for the private sector to manage better the problem of correlated risks.[12] As understanding of the underlying geology in California has improved, it has become clear that there are numerous fault lines in the state, some of which are more prone to movement than others. Moreover, understanding of the effects of different types of earthquakes on buildings has also significantly increased in recent years. For example, damage from movement of a strike/slip fault is fairly predictable, though damage from a thrust fault is less predictable. Finally, one of the most important facts that has emerged from geologic and engineering research is that the type of soil or rock on which a building is built dramatically affects the severity of loss that follows a quake of a given magnitude. Buildings constructed on landfill, for example, are subject to violent shaking because of a phenomenon known as liquefaction, in which the underlying soil behaves like Jell-O shaking in a bowl. By contrast, buildings built on bedrock are much less vulnerable to destruction or serious damage. This more detailed knowledge of earthquakes and their effects on structures makes possible more fine-grained risk assessments, which in turn make those risks more easily insurable in a purely

12. For a discussion of these studies of earthquake damage, see Ross, "Earthquake Insurance Protection in California," in Kunreuther and Ross, *Paying the Price*, pp. 67–95; and Epstein, "Catastrophic Response," pp. 294–95.

private insurance market. If companies were free to cancel policies, they would redistribute their book of business over different fault lines and over different types of structures. This would significantly diminish the problem of correlated risks.

What about the adverse selection problem? This problem arises for a type of insurance policy when there are informational asymmetries: specifically, the insureds know more about their risks than the insurers do. Poor risks flock to the policy and good risks shun it, which is an unsustainable situation in a private insurance market. As rates are raised, the good risks drop out, leaving beneficial exchanges between them and insurance companies unconsummated. This is part of the reason private firms left the market for flood insurance in the 1920s. As noted above, however, the government has developed the tools to deal with this problem. The FIRMs developed by NFIP for the entire nation have made it possible to get a better idea of what actuarially fair rates would be for various structures and properties that are at risk of flooding, and this knowledge has been partially reflected in NFIP's rate structure. One well-known problem with the current system is that government has been reluctant to apply fully the knowledge gained from the FIRMs since it continues to subsidize implicitly the cost of premiums for "grandfathered" structures that are at high risk of flood damage. A purely private market would undoubtedly apply that knowledge more fully by canceling policies and raising premium rates.

Because of the legal mandates, it is less clear how much of an adverse selection problem would exist in Florida's homeowners' insurance market and in California's earthquake insurance market if they were deregulated. Nevertheless, knowledge of the relevant risk factors does not seem to be systematically skewed toward homeowners and away from insurers, a necessary condition for an adverse selection problem. In both California and Florida, the major risk factor is the structure's location relative to the occurrence of the adverse event (epicenters for quakes and landfalls for hurricanes); in both cases, the relevant knowledge is now probably more readily available to insurers than to insured. To the extent that some structures are, by virtue of their construction, more vulnerable than others, one would expect that insurance companies would impose their own "building codes," either by denying coverage to noncompliant structures or by granting premium reductions for mitigation measures.

As Howard Kunreuther has explained, essentially two conditions must be met for a risk to be insurable by the private sector:[13] insurers must be able to (1) identify and quantify the chances of an adverse event and the extent of losses they might face, and (2) set premiums to cover claims and make a profit. In the past, condition 1 has been difficult to satisfy for natural disasters because they are relatively infrequent, which means that historical data have not been a good basis for prediction. Recently, however, scientific advances in catastrophe modeling, which includes the sciences of geology, hydrology, meteorology, and structural engineering, have greatly increased the ability to quantify the chances of various adverse events, though pockets of ambiguity remain (e.g., the extent of damage caused by thrust-fault quakes is relatively unpredictable). Regarding condition 2, to set premiums at profitable levels, it is necessary for insurance companies to be able to control for adverse selection and moral hazard. Moral hazard can be controlled by the usual instrumentalities of premium reductions for mitigation measures, deductibles, and copayments that push some of the costs of risky behavior onto policyholders. The FIRMs developed by the government can be used to limit the adverse selection problem in the case of flood insurance. For earthquakes and hurricanes, this

---

13. Howard Kunreuther, "Insurability Conditions and the Supply of Coverage," in Kunreuther and Ross, *Paying the Price*, pp. 17–50.

problem, to the extent that it exists, can be addressed in light of the scientific advances just alluded to.

THE CASE FOR PRIVATIZING
CATASTROPHE INSURANCE

One obvious difficulty with any proposal to privatize fully the provision of catastrophe insurance is that not everyone would be able to get coverage or to get coverage at affordable rates. In the near term, many property owners would have their policies canceled, and although some of them would eventually be able to get insurance with another carrier as companies redistribute their books of business, not everyone would. The reasons for this are various. In California, buildings constructed before 1940 were not built to an earthquake-resistant code, and their replacement value is a multiple of their actual market value. Insurance companies would probably not want to touch these properties. Other properties might be "theoretically" insurable but are relatively isolated or pose special, hard-to-identify risks, or high costs are associated with developing, marketing, or servicing policies in these areas. For similar reasons, some properties at high risk for hurricane damage and/or flood damage would also be uninsurable. Another likely consequence is that some insurance policies would offer more limited coverage and/or higher deductibles. On the other hand, denial of coverage would have some salutary consequences. One is to make mitigation measures more financially attractive. Bolting a wood frame house to its foundation costs a few thousand dollars but can result in huge savings in the event of an earthquake. Studies have shown that people do not apply simple cost-benefit rules to the decision to take mitigation measures, but if insurance companies offered premium reductions to those who take these measures, people would be more inclined to act prudently. Indeed, some of these measures could be financed by loans paid for through insurance premium savings. A second salutary consequence is that, if and when uninsured structures are destroyed by adverse events, a powerful message would be sent to those planning to build in high-risk areas. Development in parts of California, Florida, and in major floodplains across the country would undoubtedly be slowed and redirected away from the riskiest areas.

A fully privatized market in catastrophe insurance does what a regime of private property rights does best: it imposes the burdens of property ownership on those who make decisions regarding that property. By contrast, in the current regime, if a family builds a second home on the Gulf Coast in Florida, the state turns around and forces insurance company stockholders, other insurance policyholders, and taxpayers to subsidize that decision. If a farmer in the Midwest continues to farm land that is at risk for flooding, under the current system he can force taxpayers to pay two-thirds of his insurance premium and/or pay for rebuilding structures on the property again and again. This is before he gets payments for his crop losses.

There is no denying there would be gaps in the nation's insurance profile that do not exist now since some people who want catastrophe insurance would be unable to get it because no one would insure their structures. In addition, some property owners would be able to get it but would be too poor to afford it (however one understands that notion), though this group is unlikely to be too large, since these people are, after all, property owners. Let us call all those who cannot get insurance or cannot afford it because they are poor, the "deserving uninsured." On the other hand, there would be property owners who would be able to get insurance but not at price they are willing to pay and not because they are too poor. They may want it in the abstract, but they are not willing to pay the market rate for it.

Currently, many homeowners in California fit this description; they are interested in earthquake insurance but decline to purchase it when they discover the high deductible, exclusions, and relatively high premium. We could call those who are unwilling to purchase insurance, "undeserving uninsured," but a more neutral term would be "self-insured."

The relative sizes of the deserving uninsured and the self-insured are unknown, in part because the notion of being "too poor" to afford insurance is vague and indeterminate. In considering what should be done about both groups, the parallels with the welfare problem and welfare reform are striking and obvious. Some people cannot find work, and some choose not to work for the prevailing wage for which employment is available; the relative size of these groups is unknown. The central question regarding welfare used to be: What level and what forms of aid should those without a job get? Welfare reformers in the mid-1990s reconceived the problem in different terms: How should people be weaned off welfare? For catastrophe insurance and disaster assistance, the questions policymakers have asked throughout the second half of the twentieth century was, How can affordable insurance be made available to all and how can those without insurance be helped? The main question for the twenty-first century by contrast should be, How can people be weaned off insurance welfare? Just as welfare had the unfortunate consequence of encouraging undesirable patterns of behavior, so too current government catastrophe policies encourage undesirable behaviors in the face of disaster risks—a classic moral hazard problem. Development in high-risk areas proceeds apace, and mitigation and indeed even insurance are ignored. The idea that everyone should have affordable insurance or be given government handouts if they cannot—or choose not to—get it may be as obsolete as the idea that everyone should have a guaranteed minimum income.

It is beyond the scope of this chapter to propose a comprehensive disaster policy, but some aspects of a more attractive alternative to the status quo can be sketched. In this alternative, some elements of current policies would remain in force if for no other reason than that they are politically impossible to remove. Immediate aid to all disaster victims in the form of food, clothing and shelter would be an instance of this. The private sector might be able to handle these immediate needs (as indeed it did up until the mid–twentieth century), but no rich society is going to keep the government entirely out of the business of emergency relief. There is room to maneuver, however, in the area of long-term assistance. Political support for bailing out stricken property owners, most of whom are not poor, is waning as costs rise. A sound policy that does not encourage victims to "rebuild their lives" in a way that leaves them vulnerable to a similar disaster down the road may be politically feasible. The touchstone of any such policy must be that it does not replace private insurance that is, or could become, available. Grants and subsidized loans to property owners, qua property owners, should be eliminated since they make private insurance less attractive and are morally indefensible.

The crucial difficulty facing any such policy is the problem of credible commitment. For any more completely privatized alternative policy to work, it would be necessary for the federal government to make a credible commitment to a no-bailout policy for property owners when disaster strikes. There is no completely satisfactory solution to this problem since, short of a constitutional amendment, there is no way to guarantee that future Congresses and presidents will not give property owners a free insurance policy after the fact when disaster strikes. There is, however, a way to make that more difficult. Suppose the government periodically required each property owner to do one of three things: (1) prove that they have a catastrophe insurance policy that covers the kinds of disasters government usually addresses with supplementary appropriations bills, (2) prove that they have gone to one or more companies and gotten a quote for such a policy (which would undoubtedly include a sales pitch) and declined to purchase it, or

(3) gone to one or more companies who are writing policies in that area and gotten a letter saying that the company would not insure the property. Suppose now that Congress also passed a law that somehow committed the government to a no-bailout policy after a certain date, say five years from passage. This would allow the private sector time to reconfigure itself to take over what insurance it could, and it would allow enough time for the deserving uninsured (i.e., those who cannot get insurance or cannot afford it) to sell their property to those who are better positioned to bear the risks of being uninsured or who can afford the insurance. Perhaps real estate companies would form for this purpose; they could buy a diversified portfolio of these properties at a discount and rent them out to those who can make good use of them (including former owners). To be sure, the undeserving uninsured would get less for their property if it could not be insured (which would give them an incentive to be diligent in searching for insurance if they consider selling their property), but this would more accurately reflect its value than is currently the case because of the hidden subsidies that government bailouts represent. Cutting off these subsidies, with advance notice, is a way of bringing to bear on those who make decisions about the uses of property the consequences of those decisions.

As a result of this policy the undeserving uninsured would have sold out, found insurance after all, or chosen to continue to accept the risks they face. That is, they would have gotten out of harm's way, joined the ranks of the insured, or joined the ranks of the self-insured. Even without the influx of these individuals, the self-insured is likely to be a fairly large group, if current conditions are any guide. Fully one-third of homeowners in California do not carry CEA earthquake policies. And while NFIP participation rates have been going up, only about half the people for whom flood insurance makes sense have such a policy. If participation patterns for earthquake and flood insurance are any guide, it is likely that if hurricane coverage were to be optional for homeowners, many would choose not to buy it because it is not worth it to them. On the other hand, lenders might require this form of coverage as a condition of any loan secured by the property (though many retirees in Florida and elsewhere own their homes outright).

This proposal makes it clear to everyone, property owners and taxpayers alike, that people have faced and dealt with their risks voluntarily. It might also solve the problem of credible commitment because it would be harder for politicians to give a public justification for bailing out those without insurance in the event of a catastrophe.[14] The new members of the self-insured would have explicitly forsaken insurance or have had time to sell their property and in effect move to higher ground. In the event of a disaster, representatives from affected areas would have a much more difficult time justifying in a public forum a taxpayer-funded bailout of people who could have avoided the long-term problems they are now facing. Although immediate emergency assistance would continue to be available in the event of a catastrophe, longer term assistance aimed at restoring the status quo ante would not be.

Whether or not a proposal like this is ultimately feasible, it is facile to dismiss efforts to privatize catastrophe insurance as politically impossible and pessimistic to suppose that such efforts are unlikely to succeed in changing behavior. As costs have risen and the extent of subsidies grown, congressional representatives of unaffected areas have become increasingly reluctant to continue to support these bailouts. A long-term plan to phase out insurance welfare, considered at an appropriate time (*viz.*, not during a catastrophe), might not face the kind of organized opposition that or-

14. It also means that it does not matter too much if it is difficult to enforce the requirement to get insurance, a quote, or a letter saying no insurance can be purchased. If people choose to ignore this requirement, it would have the same implications for the voluntariness of their choices and for the public debate that is bound to arise when disaster strikes.

dinarily arises when a government subsidy is threatened, in part because the victims of future disasters do not know who they are. Also, studies have shown that many people take a "it-can't-happen-to-me" attitude toward low probability–high impact events, such as natural disasters.[15]

As to the likelihood that such a policy would be successful in changing behavior, in recent years the government has made major structural changes in welfare for the poor in a way that encourages personal responsibility. If the government can force poor people to take more responsibility for their lives, they ought to be able to force property owners, most of whom are not poor, to take more responsibility for their lives.

The limited success of welfare reform also provides reason to be optimistic about the chances for success of a program that substantially eliminates insurance welfare. Those on public assistance have had their lives devastated by a system of incentives that encouraged irresponsible behavior across many areas of their lives, and yet there are signs that changes in financial incentives have markedly affected their behavior. Changing the behavior of people on insurance welfare should be a much more tractable problem since, as property owners, they are likely to have had more experience in accepting personal responsibility for their choices.

15. See Risa Palm, "Demand for Disaster Insurance: Residential Coverage," in Kunreuther and Ross, *Paying the Price*, pp. 51–66.

CHAPTER TWO

Dealing with
Natural Disaster:
Role of the Market

Barun S. Mitra

NATURAL CALAMITIES HAVE been stalking humanity since the dawn of civilization. Natural phenomena in their myriad forms have periodically decimated the population on the planet. Primarily due to the slow killers such as droughts and diseases or sudden calamities such as floods and earthquakes, human population stayed stable at about a few million throughout much of history. Only in the last two millennia has the population begun to increase, shooting up in the past few centuries, as a result of unprecedented economic development. Economic development, coupled with scientific and technological innovations, has increasingly insulated mankind from the vagaries of nature.

Yet in recent years we have been hearing about the rising costs of natural disasters, particularly highlighted by the insurance industry, environmental organizations, and relief agencies like the Red Cross. The United Nations declared the 1990s the International Decade for Natural Disaster Reduction. Clearly it is important to get the facts right. It is even more important to keep the perspective right because it helps draw the appropriate response to the issue. In this chapter I attempt to outline the long-term trends of impacts of natural disasters, then outline a perspective, and finally highlight the range of responses that have evolved in dealing with disasters.

My conclusion is as follows: Economic development is the best protection against natural cataclysms. Government intervention in the economy has adversely affected economic growth and retarded people's ability to effectively mitigate the impact of natural hazards. To the extent that market forces has been allowed the space to operate, a whole range of options has evolved to predict, prevent, and offset the costs of these hazards.

WHAT IS A NATURAL DISASTER?

The term *natural disaster* cannot be applied to all major natural events; it can only be applied to something that has suffered some adverse consequences from a natural hazard. *Natural cataclysms* are major natural phenomena that have been part and parcel of the planet Earth since its beginning. Natural disasters, on the other hand, prove disastrous to people (similar events in uninhabited parts of the world would not be called disasters).

From this classification it would seem that, irrespective of the scale of any specific natural geologic or weather-related phenomena, if the impact on human societies is progressively decreasing, other factors are responsible.

WHAT IS THE HISTORICAL TREND?

The history of human civilization encompasses a struggle to escape from the clutches of various vagaries of nature: disease, famine, floods, droughts, heat, cold, windstorms, earthquakes, volcanic eruptions, cyclones, tornadoes, tsunamis, fire, and the like. Historical documents contain many references to the havoc caused by such calamitous events, although the chronology of such events is rather sketchy. Time has eroded memory. For instance, even the loss of the city of Pompeii in A.D. 79 was all but forgotten until archaeological discoveries about two hundred years ago substantiated what had been mythological tales. Clearly, for embattled humankind, striving to escape the clutches of nature on almost a daily basis, a natural disaster was not unique. In the midst of a continuous stream of hazards, the ones that remained etched in the collective memory were events of truly epic proportions such as the biblical flood.

The literature of ancient India has many references to droughts and famines, with authors recounting the attendant horror stories in some detail. The first major historical record of a drought in India, however, took place in Kashmir in the years A.D. 917–918. According to historical records, corpses filled the Jhelum River as people died in huge numbers and no one was left to carry out the last rites for the dead.[1]

Since then, the records of drought and famine in India in the past millenium have been quite detailed. Over the past century there are precise records of the havoc caused by the shortfall in rain, crop losses, impact on prices, and estimates of the number of people affected.

Two conclusions can be drawn from these data. One is that record keeping has greatly improved over the centuries and that the increasing reports of drought reflect this trend, rather than any real increase in the incidence of drought. Two, the impact of drought has been lessening over the century, despite higher reported incidence. This is best illustrated by the fact that, as late as the 1920s, India's population actually decreased, due to combined effects of drought and disease, for the last and only time in this century. Clearly, the Indian population, with all its poverty, has

1. A. Loveday, *The History of Economics of Indian Families* (London: G. Bell and Sons, 1914), p. 11.

nevertheless succeeded in insulating itself from one of the worst natural hazards. No mean achievement that.

Compare this with reports of major droughts in many parts of the country in the years 1999–2000. Media had to struggle to find stories of deprivation; despite their best efforts they could not find deaths that could be reasonably attributed to this drought. (The role of the media in propagating disaster will be looked into later.)

The Indian experience is not unique; it is only the latest. For instance, the early European settlers in North America could barely survive the climate and had to thank the indigenous population for helping them tide things over, thereby giving birth to the uniquely North American festival of Thanksgiving. The United States has come a long way from those precarious days. Today, even a major drought, even while destroying crops in many areas, has hardly any impact on the prices of food products. Consequently, the population has acquired complete immunity from drought.

In Europe, there is hardly any scope for a repeat of the Irish potato famine. Agricultural science has advanced so that even a nonnative plant like the potato has been successfully adopted in India; today India is one of the world leaders in potato production.

The trend is virtually the same for every kind of natural hazard. The San Francisco earthquake in 1906 and the ensuing fire destroyed millions of dollars in property and had a death toll that ranged between four to six thousand. The death toll in the last major earthquake in the California area was barely a fraction of that.

Over the past century in the United States, the annual death toll from floods has fallen from over a thousand to less than a hundred in the past few decades. Six to eight thousand people, almost a fifth of the population, perished in the hurricane that hit the small town of Galveston in 1900 and damaged property worth about $400 million in current value. In contrast, the death toll from Hurricane Andrew in 1992 was less than fifty, even though Andrew was the most destructive storm yet to hit the United States and the estimated cost of damage was upward of $17 billion.[2]

For economically less developed regions of the world, the trend is quite similar, although not as dramatic. A strong tropical storm in the Indian subcontinent, in the nineteenth century and even in the twentieth century, could leave tens of thousands dead. Nevertheless, the annual death toll from floods in countries like India has been falling, from tens of thousands in the earlier decades to a couple of thousand today. Being poor, the cost of damage to property is, of course, much lower.

One can draw the following conclusion from this trend in the richer and poorer countries. When societies are poor, they are ill-equipped to deal with natural hazards and therefore pay a much higher cost in terms of lives lost. As societies become richer, the loss of lives due to natural hazards tends to fall and the economic cost of damage to rise.

The absolute cost of damage, however, is not a good indicator, because values of property in richer societies will by definition have to be higher. For international comparison, a better figure is the ratio of damage due to natural hazards as a share of the gross national product in particular countries. The International Red Cross occasionally publishes such data in its annual *World Disaster Reports*. From these it can be seen that, in richer countries, this ratio is typically lower than in poorer countries.[3] (Some of the island nations are exceptions to this because of their higher incidence of exposure to certain kinds of disasters.)

Most recent disaster reports point out that 95 percent of deaths from natural hazards occur in poorer countries. But a look at the

2. Munich Re Group, *Natural Catastrophes—the Current Position: Topics 2000* (München, Germany: Munich Re Group, 1999).

3. Red Cross, *World Disaster Report—1997* and *World Disaster Report—1999* (Geneva, Switzerland: International Red Cross and Red Crescent Societies, 1997, 1999).

cost of natural hazards as a share of GNP shows that poorer countries bear much higher costs relative to their smaller economies. (The poor, of course, are most vulnerable.)

With improved agricultural techniques, humankind has been able to contain to a significant extent the perpetual threat of drought and famine. Likewise, improved understanding of health and hygiene has almost removed the threat of epidemics that were the worst killers. If pockets of population are still vulnerable to famine and epidemics, it is primarily due to the kind of policies pursued by these societies, rather than any peculiar natural hazards.

The trend is the same in the case of other natural phenomena such as earthquakes, eruptions, storms, and so on. The higher the level of economic development, the lower the threat from natural hazards.

WHY DO WE CONTINUE TO PERCEIVE
NATURAL HAZARDS AS THREATS?

If the trend is so clear, and the relationship with development so unequivocal, why does the perception of threat continue to dominate discussions on natural disasters? The answer may lie partly in the way we perceive change, and partly in the groups that have an interest in perpetuating a sense of crisis. Let's look at the first part of the reason. We seem to perceive events and ideas by contrast. When disasters were a constant companion of humanity, they didn't stand out. In contrast, the rare good times have been retained in the collective memory. This perhaps explains the universal appeal of the golden past, although all the evidence points to the fact that such a past was more a myth than a reality.

Today, when mankind has never had it so good, the fear of a disaster is much more pervasive, perhaps because, when most people today are safe from the vagaries of nature, the few who fail to escape stand out in sharp contrast; as a result, these fewer instances have come to dominate the discussion. This trend is reflected in the popular media. In India, for instance, the media quickly dubbed the drought in 2000 as the worst of the century and struggled to identify even one victim, while quietly forgetting the past famines that cost the lives of millions. This perception assumes a greater significance because it shapes our responses to natural hazards.[4]

WHAT IS THE ROLE OF GOVERNMENTS?

Just as disasters have been with us from the beginning, so too has been our struggle to deal with them. One of the earliest Indian texts on governance, Kautilya's *Arthashastra*, written some two thousand years ago, around the time Alexander reached the gates of India, suggests that state granaries be opened to the needy in times of crisis and that private holdings be confiscated to feed the hungry.[5] Conscientious rulers did what they could to relieve the suffering. Although the frequencies of such calamities are not known, poor communications meant that even the most well-intentioned kings could only do so much. Consequently, when droughts or famine struck, the result was often disastrous. The problems were often compounded by misrule, heavy taxation, and forced labor.

Historical texts also recognized the possibility of the moral hazards of state-sponsored charity. One suggests that relief should be offered as a loan to the people, with an obligation to return it to

---

4. "Perception by contrast"—this is like the "man bites dog" phenomena. Although very infrequent, the phenomena attract great attention because the unique event stands out in contrast to the much more common occurrences— that of people bitten by dogs. The latter remain almost invisible because it doesn't stand out in general perception.

5. A. L. Basham, *The Wonder That Was India: A Survey of the History and Culture of the Indian Sub-Continent before the Coming of the Muslims* (New Delhi, India: Rupa & Co., 1981), p. 192.

the state in the years when going is better.[6] During later periods modern concepts such as food for work or workfare rather than welfare were practiced in some areas. There are other historical examples of rulers engaging a large workforce in times of famine and crisis to build large monuments and palaces, which had very little functional value but provided some relief to the workers and their families.

In times of crisis, poor communication, transport, and storage facility reduced the efforts of the most energetic rulers to symbolic gestures, meaning that private agencies and charities probably played a greater role in dealing with a crisis in their immediate vicinities. But because of its diffused character, this activity has not received the kind of attention that it deserved. Again perception by contrast focused attention on what the state did or did not do, rather than on what the people could and did do to mitigate the hardships.

In our times, this role of the state in times of crisis has become almost a touchstone for determining the state's legitimacy. Of course, even in ancient times, many rulers had the foresight to seek legitimacy from their subjects, and disaster relief was a visible way in which the kings could legitimize their administrations.

In more democratic times, politicians seek to legitimize their role by offering similar patronage to their constituencies. As Amartya Sen has pointed out, democratic governance, along with a relatively free media, has played its part in mitigating some of the worst effects of natural disasters.[7] Democratic India has a much better record in dealing with droughts and famine than either its colonial masters or its feudal predecessors. Competitive politics, along with pressure from the media, has by and large ensured that the state

6. Mohinuddin Alamgir, *Famine in South Asia* (Cambridge, Mass.: Oelgeschlager, Gunn, & Haine Publishers, 1980), p. 56.

7. Jean Dreze and Amartya Sen, *India: Economic Development and Social Opportunity* (New Delhi, India: Oxford University Press, 1995), p. 76.

agencies have acted early enough to prevent the development of full-scale famines.

Likewise, long before the advent of the welfare state, even feudal and colonial states recognized that, in times of emergency, measures (other than charity) such as food for work, providing citizens an opportunity to work, and similar efforts are often more effective in helping the needy.

THE IMPACT OF STATE INTERVENTION

In times of major crises, it is natural to look to the largest or the most powerful or the most visible organization. The organs of the state or government have logically fit that bill from the earliest times. The "invisible hand" of the market, after all, is rarely deemed capable of dealing with such visible crises.

Accepting the role of the state in times of natural calamities, however, comes with certain other costs. First, the entry of the state as the most visible agent only reinforces our mode of perception by contrast, no matter how distorted the actual picture may be from this perception. Second, once the role of the state comes to the center stage, various other measures that people have been taking to mitigate the disaster's effects go out of fashion. On the one hand, this intervention by the state distorts the scope of the market in dealing with natural catastrophe. On the other hand, there is a scramble to seek political favors to get relief and rehabilitation benefits, which in turn triggers the politics of patronage, with political establishments and their constituencies vying to corner a greater share of the public pie.

Thus, both the United States, one of the richest countries, and India, one of the poorest, have in the past few decades declared an increasing number of natural catastrophes as natural disasters in order to gain political mileage. Historically, the number of people actually affected by natural disasters has fallen, but political intervention has created the opposite impression, leading to the justification of this tendency, contrary to actual experience. This political intervention has in turn diverted attention from the various private initiatives that have evolved but that, by their nature, are diffused and many times location-specific.

This is best seen in contemporary discussions on methods to mitigate natural disasters. The literature is dominated by technological quick fixes. For instance, there has been much focus on building codes and earthquake-proofing of various structures. Of course, the most vulnerable people can afford only shanties, meaning that, for them, such technological solutions are rarely if ever practical.

More seriously, such efforts could lead to even greater tragedies if these panaceas fail in the face of a natural calamity. The 1989 earthquake in the then Soviet republic of Armenia not only left tens of thousands dead but also reportedly destroyed many buildings, particularly those built during the Soviet era. This highlights the clear danger of legalizing mandatory standards in the hope of promoting safety. First, if the standards are sanctioned by state agencies, then there is little incentive to improve on the existing standards. But, even mort important, should these standards fail at some point in the face of some natural hazard, the impact will be much more widespread and devastating.

Discussion on protection from natural calamity also focuses on preserving the local ecosystems in the hope that these will act as barriers to some forms of calamities like floods or cyclones. This may look sustainable and a cheaper alternative, but in reality this discussion on ecology too is more often than not quite off the mark. Take the case of flooding in the coastal areas. Every year thousands die, particularly in the developing countries, due to tropical cyclones that hit the coastal settlements.

Would the natural mangroves and other ecological barriers be more effective in reducing damage? Not if one looks back at history. One of the areas most vulnerable to tropical storms is the

Gangetic delta between India and Bangladesh. A storm in this region in 1864 left more than 70,000 people dead in and around the city of Calcutta. In 1876, the toll in Bengal was 200,000. At that time, the much-valued mangroves were at their pristine best. Yet the destruction was far in excess of the current average. Clearly, the focus on ecological barriers is no panacea.

Intervention by state agencies also poses other kinds of hazards. The problem of moral hazards of state intervention in disaster relief was recognized by President Grover Cleveland of the United States who, denying federal aid to some drought-stricken counties in 1887, wrote that "federal aid in such cases encourages the expectation of paternal care on the part of the government and weakens the sturdiness of our national character, while it prevents the indulgence among our people of that kindly sentiment and conduct which strengthens the bonds of common brotherhood."[8] But what is not usually recognized is that there are other serious social consequences of such well-meaning interventions.

The race for political patronage inevitably increases the prospect for corruption in distribution of relief and management of rehabilitation programs. Virtually every major natural calamity in India has been followed by reports of mismanagement and corruption. What is worse is that political intervention also politicizes the flow of information. Depending on the circumstance, political establishments may seek to blame nature, political opponents, other government agencies, or even the people for the disaster. There is also a tendency to play the crisis up or down in the hope of gaining political mileage. The result of all this is distortion in the flow of information, making the management of the crisis even more difficult. The victims, of course, are worse off as they get kicked like a political football. Truth is the natural casualty in this process.

8. John W. Sommer, "Disaster Unlimited," *The Freeman*, April 1986, pp. 134–38.

The supercyclone that hit the coast of the eastern Indian state of Orissa in November 1999 left more than ten thousand people dead (unofficial reports put the figure at more than double that number). The media reported that the Central Government in Delhi was reluctant to seek international help as it might reflect on the credibility of the national government, despite the fact that, even two weeks after the tragedy, many villages remained cut off, with no information coming out or relief reaching the survivors.[9]

Discussions on moral hazard are generally restricted to the impact of state-sponsored relief on the recipients and the victims. But even donor agencies are not immune. For instance, state governments of regions affected by a natural calamity often claim that things are under control and that everything that could be done is being done to help the victims. At the same time, the same governments often make grossly inflated claims of loss when seeking help from the central government. In many instances, the local agencies fail to spend the money allocated to them for disaster relief.

This process of politicization leaves a long trail. For instance, one of the first impacts of state-sponsored rehabilitation is to enable the survivors to rebuild virtually the same structures at the same spot, leaving the population again vulnerable to a similar tragedy next time round.

This process of politicization is the same in developed countries. For example, in the United States, in many states property developers and insurance companies seek political protection at the cost of others. In areas prone to natural hazards, insurance premiums tend to go higher. But this normal economic practice is seen as bad for business by the property developers because it could raise the cost of their property and deter prospective buyers. The govern-

9. S. Parasuraman and P. V. Unnikrishnan, eds., *India's Disaster Reports: Towards a Policy Initiative* (New Delhi, India: Oxford University Press, 2000), pp. 199–200.

ment would of course like to balance the two interests. But the result is that a decision that could have been taken in the marketplace by buyers and sellers now becomes a political football, and it is the ordinary consumers who must bear the additional costs.[10]

Another form of threat arises out state-sponsored charity. State intervention distorts the social fabric. In times of crisis, the natural tendency of many members of society is to try and help those affected. But when the state takes on that responsibility, it destroys the fellowship and camaraderie among citizens. Since the state seeks to take the prime responsibility to mitigate the effects of disasters, achieving this through universal taxation, citizens feel that they no longer have any need to be involved in the process of relief and rehabilitation.

In India, in the 1960s and even in the 1970s, a natural disaster in one part of the country evoked enormous sympathy in other parts. Even with poor communications, people followed events closely. Thousands of volunteers from political and nonpolitical organizations went from house to house collecting money and any other kind of relief material possible. Today, live commentaries from disaster zones evoke hardly a cursory glance. It is not uncommon to hear people say that, if the government is collecting taxes to help people in distress, no further assistance should be needed.

COMPETITIVE POLITICS AND THE ROLE OF THE MEDIA

Competitive politics, particularly that manifested in democratic societies, coupled with a free media, has shaped not only the way a natural calamity is perceived but also the response.

Competitive politics has meant that the establishment in power

10. Scott E. Harrington, "Rethinking Disaster Policy," *Regulation* 23, no. 1 (April 2000): 40–46.

constantly has to look over its shoulder to see whether its political opponents are trying to discredit it. No issue creates a groundswell of public opinion like that of natural disasters and the plight of victims. It is indeed no coincidence that the spread of democratic governance has over the past hundred years significantly contributed to minimizing the impact of one of the worst natural scourges—famine.[11] This explains the different experiences of India and China in the 1950s and 1960s. Famines and devastation on the scale witnessed in China did not develop in India. The political will to get people and material to the affected regions has come, to a substantial extent, from political pressures. The presence of relatively free media has also contributed to this development by bringing to light the tragic aftermath of a disaster, highlighting the human plight, and helping mobilize resources to deal with the immediate crisis.

However, the focus of this analysis rests on the role played by the state in alleviating a crisis. Not surprisingly, this analysis takes attention away from the historical trends of the impact of natural disaster, including the role of economic development in mitigating the impacts of natural calamities, the role of the various local and private initiatives in dealing with a crisis, and the evolution of various economic tools under the market system that made many of the disaster-mitigation techniques affordable.

Most important, this focus on state agencies as prime players in disaster mitigation also led to the growth of the disaster interests. The competitive politics and free media that helped highlight the aftermath of a natural calamity also fueled the interest groups' lobbying for an ever larger share of the relief and rehabilitation pie.[12]

11. Jean Dreze and Amartya Sen, *Hunger and Public Action* (New Delhi, India: Oxford University Press, 1989), pp. 257–79.

12. Kuldeep Mathur and Niraja G. Jayal, *Drought, Policy and Politics: The Need for a Long Term Perspective* (New Delhi, India: Sage Publications, 1993), pp. 97–125.

In this tussle, the interests of ordinary citizens affected by the disaster often get lost.

Ironically, increased political competition along with faster modes of communication have tended to aggravate the problem. Improved communication brings live coverage of natural disasters to people in all corners of the world; political competition brings them to center stage. But this flow of information and analysis more often than not seems to have hindered our understanding of the issue and colored our perception of the events. For instance, advances in information technology have magnified the current calamities by overwhelming reportage. As a result, our perception is distorted and an impression is created that the situation is getting worse.

This development makes a mockery of real historical trends. The relatively few surviving records of historical catastrophes are cited as evidence that natural disasters were less severe in the past. In contrast almost daily reports of natural disasters affecting one or another part of the contemporary world are taken as evidence that people today may be exposed to a greater degree of natural hazards. Thus, the frequency of reports is being misinterpreted as incidence of events. This misinterpretation shows how competitive politics and free media are both prone to perception by contrast and therefore contribute to political interventions that at best may be unnecessary and at worst give rise to politics of patronage. Two sets of errors have contributed to this distortion. One is the nature and role of government. Second is the capacity of the market to respond to such calamities.

THE ROLE OF GOVERNMENT

The basic purpose of the state is to protect the rights, liberty, and property of its citizens. A representative government derives its legitimacy from the consent of the governed, under the assumption that the state organs will place their use of coercive force under an objective set of laws. Using state powers to tax all citizens to provide relief to the victims of disaster raises the prospect of some people seeking protection at the cost of others. The rise of the disaster lobby, and the rapid growth in the number of events that the political establishment declares as disasters to qualify for one kind of relief or another, is actually a manifestation of the process of the politicization of disaster management.

If one accepts the classical liberal tradition of political theory, and recognizes the limited role of government in protecting the rights of the citizens from domestic criminals and foreign conquerors (that is, the basic police and military functions), then the question is how to interpret a natural calamity.

Should a natural calamity be seen as a disaster when citizens are affected and therefore the state called in? The state agencies are not usually called in to protect and rehabilitate single individuals who may be affected by a natural disaster. For instance, a lightning strike on a private home normally does not evoke the same response from the state agencies as a tornado or a cyclone ripping through large areas, destroying many lives and damaging many properties. But should mere differences in scale justify different responses from state agencies? Could it be said that this difference in scale disrupts the normal private processes, social and economic, and that only the state organs are large enough to deal with a crisis of such magnitude?

If one keeps the fundamental role of government in mind, and does not look at state power as primarily a tool for redistributing resources through political intervention, then the role of the state in dealing with natural calamities will become clear. Just as the state agencies are entrusted with protecting rights, liberty, and property from criminals and aggressors, so too the state agencies must try to reduce imminent and immediate threats to life and property as a result of some natural calamity.

Just as protection against crime does not oblige the state to provide relief and ensure rehabilitation of the victim of a crime, so too a victim of a natural disaster cannot expect economic rehabilitation after the disaster. One has to perform some intellectual gymnastics to show that political intervention by the state to protect life and rights naturally extends to economic intervention to provide relief and ensure rehabilitation.

As has been argued above, intervention to redistribute resources, using the political tools of governance, is economically inefficient and ethically disastrous. Such interventions not only disrupt the ability of the marketplace to evolve a diverse range of strategies to deal with natural calamities but also reinforce the justification for state intervention for the alleged market failures. But since these market failures are primarily the result of state intervention, such interventions only draw the state agencies in to ever-deepening political quagmire. The politics of patronage and corruption is an inevitable outcome of such intervention.

SCOPE OF THE MARKET IN DISASTER MITIGATION

We must understand the historical trends and appreciate the perspective to be able to draw the right conclusions. A distorted perspective based on impressions created by the front-loaded nature of reports of natural calamities inevitably raises doubts over the ability of the markets and private initiatives to deal with the apparently increasing frequency of disasters. The only institutions that seem capable of rising to the task appear to be the agencies of the state. On the other hand, if one of the basic characteristics of progress is the increasing success in insulating populations from the vagaries of nature, then one would have to recognize the role of private initiatives in dealing with such natural crises.

First, economic development has been the single most important factor in helping to insulate humankind from the periodic havoc caused by natural elements throughout history. The significance of economic development is borne out by the fact that today the developing countries and poorer societies are much more prone to suffer nature's wrath than richer countries. According to some estimates, 95 percent of deaths from natural calamities today occur in developing countries. Richer societies, therefore, are better placed to deal with natural calamities. It seems tragic that with the increased attention to natural calamities in recent times and the declaration of the 1990s as the International Decade for Natural Disaster Reduction, the role of economic development in mitigating catastrophes gets little mention.

There has, however, been a general recognition that giving markets a free rein in many spheres of activity helps improve economic performance. In many parts of the world there is trend toward dismantling many of the legal restrictions and regulations that are thought to have restrained economic performance. But there has been little recognition of the need for economic development to secure humankind from nature's fury. Indeed, if anything there are increased calls for the state to intervene to mitigate the effects of natural disasters.

Historically, the role of the state in disaster management has been marginal, although some ancient texts do mention various strategies the agencies of the state could adopt in the face of a natural calamity. Nevertheless, the actual capacity of the state to mitigate disasters in far-flung areas was limited because of lack of communication, transportation, and facilities, coupled with a lack of economic and technological resources.

The earliest records of private initiatives to mitigate risks from disasters come from ancient Greece, Rome, and India, which show forms of insurance being used as a financial tool to offset different forms of hazards.[13] Ancient traders were among the most vulnerable

---

13. Susan L. Cutter, ed., *Environmental Risks and Hazards* (Englewood Cliffs, N.J.: Prentice-Hall, 1993), pp. 33–54.

to natural disasters, for their wealth depended on trade with distant lands. And every consignment could be lost to either some natural calamity like stormy seas or man-made hazards such as banditry. Because they risked so much, the traders were the first to try and hedge their risks by adopting various financial strategies, some of which were little more than gambling. A rich trader in those ancient times could be ruined if a ship carrying his goods were lost. (Centuries later Lloyds of London would be created out of this need to secure the increasing number of ships at sea.)

Today, of course, insurance plays a great role in mitigating risks in the face of a wide range of uncertainties. As Henry Ford reportedly said at the beginning of the twentieth century, but for insurance companies, no investor would have put his money in building New York City when one cigarette butt could have turned that investment to ashes.[14]

Despite the advances of technology and the better collection of information, however, some degree of uncertainty will always remain in all situations. Therefore there will always be the need to hedge one's risks, natural or man-made. The insurance companies, realizing this need, came up with a new form of insurance for the insurers—reinsurance, which allows insurers in one area to disperse their risks over a much larger base. Although reinsurance developed mostly in the nineteenth century with the possibility of international capital flows, elements of reinsurance have also been found in twelfth- and thirteenth-century Europe.[15]

The development of financial instruments to deal with the unforeseen natural hazards underscores the primary role of capital in alleviating some of the effects of such disasters and highlights the need for economic development to make such capital investments affordable. In the contemporary world, apart from some of the

14. Swiss Re, *An Introduction to Reinsurance* (Zurich, Switzerland: Swiss Reinsurance Company, 1996), p. 4.
    15. Ibid., pp. 3–20.

island nations, the percentage share of gross national product affected by natural disasters annually in richer nations tends to be much smaller than in poorer countries, although in absolute terms the losses in richer nations tend to be much higher than in poorer nations. Clearly, poverty means that the population is that much closer to nature's occasional fury and consequently that much more vulnerable.

Availability of capital is, of course, only a part of the story because even the best insurance policy cannot prevent a natural calamity. But this capital does make possible interventions through the development of science and technology that can increasingly predict and even prevent a natural calamity from turning into a disaster. It can also make the rescue, relief, and rehabilitation more effective.

Let's take a look at how the market, if unrestrained by state regulations, would deal with natural calamities. Economic development increases the value of property, which means that the risk of potential loss also rises. Of course, increasing property value also increases the premium that the owner has to pay for any kind of insurance. The property owner can thus decide whether to pay a higher premium for building in an area more prone to natural hazards or to adopt measures that would make his building more secure against the hazards or to move to a safer location. Insurance companies and other stakeholders evaluate a similar range of options in order to ensure that their propositions remain attractive to the property owners.

In a competitive market, there is constant pressure on insurance companies to find ways of lowering risks and thereby keeping the premiums low. In the same way, property owners have to constantly find ways of equating the benefits of higher premiums to cover the higher property value and search for other ways of lowering risks. This continuous tussle provides the impetus for searching for alternative investments to reduce the exposure to risks. And this is where advances in science and technology play a major role.[16]

For instance, take the case of weather forecasting. A century ago, forecasting was in its infancy. With the development of radar, satellites, and computers, however, weather is being tracked around the clock, all over the world. From farmers, ordinary citizens, and airlines to insurance companies, all have become serious consumers of weather bulletins. This growing demand provides a new impetus to the science of meteorology as well as new modes of communicating the information to those who need it as quickly and as appropriately as possible. A correct weather prediction, be it of rainfall, a storm, or a tornado, goes a long way in preparing to meet the crisis.

Although effective prediction can help reduce losses from a natural calamity, in many instances prediction is not yet possible (e.g., earthquakes). Advances in building sciences, structural engineering, and material sciences, however, have helped substantially reduce the risk from collapsing structures and fires in the aftermath of a major earthquake.

In other situations, such as volcanic eruptions, ability to predict may be low and possibility of lowering damage not viable. But with adequate monitoring, a certain basic level of preparedness could be maintained so as to divert the flow of the magma from a volcanic eruption and prevent the destruction of life and property. In other cases, such as avalanches, it is possible to trigger controlled explosions to disperse the buildup of snow and prevent the possible avalanche by continually monitoring the situation.

The bottom line in all this is economic development, for it enables people to adopt a wide range of measures to insulate themselves and prevent natural calamities from turning into human dis-

16. Robert M. Hamilton, "Science and Technology for Natural Disaster Reduction," *Natural Hazards Review*, February 2000, pp. 56–60.

asters. Economic development increases the value of life and property and therefore makes such financial and technological measures to reduce losses affordable. Indeed, economic development even enables private charities to mobilize much greater resources much more efficiently to reduce the suffering of victims and help them rebuild their lives.

The competitive environment of an open market provides the best incentive to all the players: the financial sectors, the weather forecasters, the scientists, the engineers, the businesses, the homeowners, and everyone striving to find better and cheaper ways of dealing with natural catastrophes. Yet there have been constant attempts by governments in most countries, particularly in this century, to intervene in the marketplace and consequently to hamper the ability of the people to deal with natural calamities effectively.

Faced with a crisis, such as a drought or famine, one of the first things state agencies do is to institute price control and restrict the movement of goods. It is thought that, by putting a ceiling on the prices of basic food products, people will have better access to these goods. What is ignored is that, in a condition of scarcity, price control achieves exactly the opposite. Without the price signal, there is no way of knowing the enormity of scarcity and therefore no incentive to move goods to the affected areas. It is no coincidence that price control in a crisis situation inevitably leads to the growth of black markets and profiteering on a level that would be impossible to sustain in free-market conditions.

Contrast this situation with the experience of richer countries in the world today. Economic development and dramatic improvements in agricultural practices have created a situation in which food production is no longer a major concern. Expenditure on food as a percentage of family income has been falling. The result is that even a major drought or a flood makes hardly a blip on the price of food products. For the first time in history many societies have reached a place where famine and hunger have all but been eliminated.

Nevertheless, the attraction of price control has continued. Restrictions on capital flows and the insurance markets reflect this desire to lower the cost of disaster mitigation through state intervention. Not unexpectedly, the results are exactly the opposite. Poor policies adopted by poorer countries have extracted a particularly heavy price. State monopoly over meteorological information has meant that there is no incentive to disseminate the information in a useful manner. Restrictions on channels of communication and state monopolies have discredited these channels to the extent that many people discount the information merely because it comes over nationalized broadcasting media. Restrictions on access to technology mean that even those who could have found the information from independent sources do not find it easy to do so. After the calamity, the thin spread of the channels of communication and technology means that few of these channels survive the disaster. This leads to a situation where even weeks after the disaster many of the affected areas remain cut off, without any relief or protection.

It could be said that many of the safety regulations, such as building codes mandated by the government and effectively enforced, particularly in developed countries, have played a significant role in mitigating the effects of natural calamities such as earthquakes or fires. Two points stand out here. One, being richer has meant that these societies have been able to afford these measures. Two, there are few reasons to think that these safety measures have been cost-effective. On the other hand it could be argued that an open market in property and real estate would have incorporated many of the safety features as part of a process of value addition and would do it in a much more cost-effective manner than the regulatory approach.

This is why more than twenty million people can afford to stay in the greater San Francisco area in California despite the possibility of an earthquake or why two million people choose to live in the shadow of Mount Vesuvius in Naples or why authorities can spend upward of $30 million to evacuate people from coastal areas in Hawaii in the face a tsunami warning. On the other hand, ten thousand people perish in sparsely populated hills of the Himalayas when the earth shakes; even greater numbers die in tropical cyclones even after the storm has been tracked for days because either people remain ignorant or they can't afford to take any precautions. Even as the worst manifestations of famines have been all but eliminated, malnutrition remains one of the most deadly but silent of all killers.

The sharp contrast between the experiences of developed countries and developing ones in the face of natural calamities of similar types and magnitude leads to only one conclusion. Economic development provides the best protection against natural hazards. A free market is much more efficient in allocating resources to meet the requirements of all participants. Disaster mitigation is a value-added product that becomes increasingly affordable in a competitive economic environment. In contrast, greater levels of government intervention in the economy not only retard economic development but also make people more vulnerable to natural calamities.

CHAPTER THREE

A
Fool's
Errand?

John Ahrens

Giving money and power to government is like giving whiskey and car keys to teenage boys.
—P. J. O'Rourke, *Parliament of Whores*

ON THE OTHER HAND . . .

If they don't want me living up here, they [FEMA] can get their checkbook out.
—Ben Boggs, resident of the Ohio floodplain[1]

THE NAME OF the key government agency—the Federal Emergency Management Administration (FEMA)—pretty much tells the story. The federal government now undertakes to manage emergencies, a task so daunting that it must call forth all the concentrated regulatory and economic power that resides in federal institutions and bureaucracies. FEMA takes the point position in this massive effort; its strategic plan recognizes a "need to lead and

---

1. Mr. Boggs was quoted in an article in the *Louisville Courier-Journal* on July 10, 2000. The article reported FEMA's threats to put Clark County, Indiana, on probation for flood insurance unless some eighty mobile homes parked in the floodplain of the Ohio River were relocated.

support the Nation in a comprehensive, risk-based emergency management program."[2]

Responding to this need will require the expenditure of enormous sums from tax revenues and the implementation of complex regulations to manage emergencies before, during, and after the fact.[3] The need for this massive effort is apparent, seemingly, in the newspapers and news broadcasts of any given day; they typically feature a litany of ongoing catastrophes—fires, floods, earthquakes, volcanic eruptions, violent weather. And the demand for this effort is certainly apparent from the same sources. Media coverage of natural disasters virtually always features a parade of victims complaining about the government's inadequate or inept or unfair response, followed by somber punditry on the government's seeming inability to shoulder this crucial responsibility. Federal management of one's emergencies has quickly become just another entitlement.

So perhaps this essay is a fool's errand. Can a society that authorizes government to respond quickly and effectively to natural disasters and other such calamities hope to preserve its liberty? Well . . . no. History—recent history, at least—speaks fairly consistently about the dangers of ceding to government the power to act on a large scale or a short timetable,[4] even—or perhaps especially—when the end in view is generally thought to be a good one. Providing emergency relief and, perhaps, reconstruction assistance to

2. "Partnership for a Safer Future: Strategic Plan FY 1998–FY 2007," Federal Emergency Management Administration, at FEMA.GOV, http://www.fema.gov/library/spln_1.htm#fore.

3. The documents on FEMA's website (www.fema.gov) are quite explicit about all of this.

4. Robert Higgs provides an excellent historical account of how emergencies, particularly economic and military emergencies, have contributed to the growth of the federal government in *Crisis and Leviathan: Critical Episodes in the Growth of American Government* (New York: Oxford University Press, 1987). Mary C. Comerio gives a succinct overview of the development of federal policy concerning natural disasters in "Paying for the Next Big One," *Issues in Science & Technology* 16, no. 3 (spring 2000): 65.

the victims of so-called natural disasters—large fires, earthquakes, floods, tornadoes and hurricanes, and other such eruptions of nature—seems an eminently good cause to many citizens of the contemporary United States. And efforts to mitigate the effects of such disasters by mandating various preventive efforts seem a natural extension.

This is so in part, I suspect, because such disasters have about them an air of randomness; there seems to be precious little that individuals can do to protect themselves, and that little is very costly. At the same time, there is a widespread conviction that market or other voluntaristic institutions will not do a very good job of responding to natural disasters. (I am inclined to agree with this, and I will suggest why I think this is so, although not at any great length, later in this essay.) This seems one of those genuinely hard cases in which a choice must be made between two genuine but conflicting values.

That is to say, it seems that we can preserve our freedom and the benefits that accompany it, or we can charge government with protecting us from one of the more intractable vicissitudes of life. And—*O tempora! o mores!*—it is no real surprise that people today clamor for protection at the expense of freedom, whether their own or someone else's. To defend freedom against the claims of victims, even to suggest that something of value is being lost in the rush to give the federal government the authority to manage emergencies, is surely a fool's errand.

This last point will play a central role in my discussion of disaster relief. That many (most) people are too willing to sacrifice freedom for security certainly is not a new phenomenon. Frederic Bastiat, writing in France during the period surrounding the Revolution of 1848, explained this willingness to sacrifice freedom to the demands of the moment in terms of a distinction between what is *seen* and what is *not seen*. Bastiat points out that "an act, a habit, an institution, a law produces not only one effect, but a series of effects."[5]

The direct and immediate consequences are easily seen, but those consequences that are more indirect, or emerge later or at a distance, are not so easily seen. And it often happens that the immediate consequences are apparently beneficial; it is only later that unfortunate consequences begin to emerge. This produces all sorts of problems for human beings and societies: "When a man is impressed by the effect *that is seen* and has not yet learned to discern the effects *that are not seen*, he indulges in deplorable habits, not only through natural inclination, but deliberately."[6]

Bastiat uses this distinction to explain many of the political and social controversies of his day, and it can equally well illuminate our discussion of disaster relief. What is *seen* in a natural disaster is the plight of victims and the immediate improvement that government can effect. What is *not seen*—indeed, what is often wilfully ignored—is the damage to freedom, and perhaps to other values, that ultimately emerges from the decision to give government the power to manage prevention, relief, and reconstruction. Security triumphs because the loss of freedom simply is not seen, or is not seen to be of sufficient importance to weigh heavily in the balance. I return to this below.

THE SLIPPERY SLOPE

On the other hand, this dilemma really cannot be that stringent. Any—*any*—grant of authority to government puts us on the slippery slope to unlimited expansion and misuse of that authority. The war on drugs is an obvious example; during the latter half of the

5. Frederic Bastiat, "What Is Seen and What Is Not Seen," in *Selected Essays on Political Economy*, ed. George B. De Huszar (Irvington-on-Hudson, N.Y.: Foundation for Economic Education, 1995), p. 1.
6. Ibid.

twentieth century and the beginning of this century, the federal government's efforts to prevent drug use have grown into a massive structure of costly programs and intrusive regulations. Children are subjected, often involuntarily, to drug education programs whose effectiveness is questionable and whose content is more so. Constitutional guarantees of due process and privacy have been seriously eroded by efforts to enforce drug laws, and many officials and citizens clamor for even further erosion of these guarantees. Regulations concerning such things as the medical use of marijuana or the cultivation of hemp, matters that have little to do with illegal drug use, restrict the freedom of individuals to pursue thoroughly legitimate ends. Hysterical sentencing policies have undermined respect for the law and driven the costs of incarceration to astronomical levels. And the practice of racial profiling has lent a racist tinge to the whole mess. It is a popular joke that the war on drugs is over and that drugs have won. The truth is that government has won, and this is no joke at all.

Certainly, our experience with ceding to government the authority to police drug use and the myriad of other so-called victimless crimes should give us pause—and equally so our experience with federal regulation of the economy in the name of the public good or economic justice or some other ideal that is often ill defined and presented as self-evident. The slippery slope is indeed slippery; perhaps we are well advised to limit government to the protection of individual rights, as John Locke, John Stuart Mill, and other traditional defenders of liberty would have us do. Unfortunately, the situation is no more encouraging when we turn our attention to the government's authority to prevent or punish *real* crimes in which an identifiable individual's rights are violated by identifiable others—crimes like assault, theft, and fraud. Due process, freedom of speech, private property, privacy, and all the other rights that comprise freedom are equally a hindrance to the regulation of personal and economic behavior *and* to the prevention of real crimes. That is why a society that aspires to freedom, such as that of the United States, surrounds authority with all sorts of constitutional and legal provisions to ensure that it does not turn against us. Hence, the danger of unlimited expansion of the government's power cannot render the issue of disaster relief especially problematic; this danger arises whenever we give government the authority to do anything.

The real issue, at least for someone who is committed to the ideal of a free society, is whether disaster relief presents us with one of those situations in which it is appropriate to confront this danger and cede some authority to government. If it does not, this would not be a unique or difficult bullet to have to bite. One can acknowledge the desirability of all sorts of things—a drug-free society, prompt help for the unfortunate, universal literacy—without being committed to making government a major or even a minor player in efforts to achieve these things. Into which category, then, does disaster relief fall?

THE STATE OF NATURE

Despite the slippery slope, the most ardent defenders of freedom are generally inclined to invest in government the authority to police violations of individual rights (well, most of them, at any rate). Anarchists, the most ardent defenders of freedom, if not the most practical, are strongly disinclined to do this. The anarchist/liberal debate is well represented in the current philosophical literature, and I will not enter that debate directly in this essay, although I do hope that my accounting of liberal arguments will show that they are an adequate response to anarchist objections.[7] In any case,

---

7. For a succinct discussion of this debate, see Aeon Skoble, "The Anarchist Controversy," in Tibor R. Machan and Douglas B. Rasmussen, eds., *Liberty for the 21st Century* (Lanham, Md.: Rowman & Littlefield, 1995).

the mainstream of the classical liberal tradition has typically recognized the necessity of government to create and maintain a structure of laws within which freedom can flourish.[8] Why is this so?

The answer to this question often emerges from a contrast between the state of nature, in which human beings live without any central authority and are each responsible for protecting themselves from force and fraud, and civil society, in which this responsibility resides solely in the hands of a central authority to which all are subject. John Locke characterizes the human condition in the state of nature as "a state of perfect freedom to order their actions and dispose of their possessions and persons as they think fit, within the bounds of the law of nature, without asking leave or depending upon the will of any other man."[9]

Our freedom is "perfect," yet it is limited even before we create government to constrain our actions. It is limited by the natural rights to life, liberty, and property prescribed by the law of nature and possessed by every human being. Locke explicates these rights in negative terms, as rights against interference, rather than rights to any sort of assistance, and makes the protection of these rights the foundation of his normative theory of government. Government is constituted to protect these rights, and government itself must respect these rights.

But Locke also argues that the state of nature, while it is a state of "perfect" freedom, is a state of some inconvenience as well. It is terribly inefficient, for there is much duplication of efforts to prevent and sanction rights violations. And this state inevitably hinders the cooperation that is essential for the production of most of the

8. I do not wish to get bogged down in labels here. By "classical liberalism" I mean simply that tradition in Western political philosophy that has made individual freedom the most significant standard by which governments and societies are to be evaluated. The relationship of this tradition to modern liberalism and conservatism is complex.

9. John Locke, *The Second Treatise of Government*, chap. 2, §4.

advantages of life; the lack of a central authority to define, investigate, and adjudicate rights violations results in uncertainty and instability and thus engenders mistrust.

Reasonable human beings (and most are reasonable) can easily see the advantage of creating such an authority and accepting the consequent restrictions on their freedom and their obligation to pay a fair share of the costs of maintaining the central authority. But they can also see the danger: this central authority can itself become a threat to the preexisting, *natural* rights to life, liberty, and property that it was constituted to protect. If all goes well, these natural rights limit the scope of centralized authority by establishing boundaries that cannot be crossed and thereby determine the scope of individual freedom. The danger is that all may not go well.

Thomas Hobbes, although himself no great proponent of individual freedom, gives an account of the movement from the state of nature to civil society that has had considerable influence on the development of the classical liberal tradition. Hobbes has a grim view of the state of nature; it is so fraught with conflict and insecurity and mistrust that the manifold benefits of cooperative endeavor are simply unattainable, and the life of man is "solitary, poor, nasty, brutish, and short." The law of nature prescribes no preexisting natural rights; it prescribes only that we do whatever is necessary to escape this situation.

What is necessary, according to Hobbes, is to submit to a government that has the power to control our aggression and thereby make cooperation the rational course. Any government that can bring some kind of order and stability to our lives, no matter how tyrannical and oppressive it may be, is preferable to the dismal state of nature.

The arguments advanced by Locke and Hobbes form two important poles in the debate concerning the scope of freedom and the limits of authority. Locke argues that freedom is mandated and defined by the preexisting natural rights that government is formed to secure; Hobbes rejects the notion of preexisting limits on authority and finds little room for freedom in his grim account of the human condition. But at a deeper level, these two views are united, for both are the result of an effort to resolve the intractable tension between human individuality and human sociality.

Human beings *are* individuals. The claims of politicians aside, I do not feel your pain. More to the point, each of us has a distinct perspective, a unique structure of values and motivations, varied prospects—in short, a different life from every other. This individuality is the ground of freedom. At the same time, we are thoroughly social creatures; our lives, our very beings are shaped by our relationships with others. An important dimension of our sociality can be described as instrumental; production of the advantages of life, material and otherwise, is much enhanced by cooperation. This is the dimension of sociality emphasized by Locke and Hobbes.

But there is another dimension as well, typified by the relationships between family members or between intimate friends. Because we are the sorts of creatures we are, we find ourselves drawn together by intellectual and emotional commitments. And many of these relationships are what might be called *constitutional*: they shape our perspectives, our values, our prospects—our being. This sociality is the ground of civil society, with its attendant restrictions on freedom.

John Stuart Mill, the great nineteenth-century defender of individual liberty, addresses this same tension, but in a quite different way. He rejects both Locke's natural-law account of freedom and Hobbes's conventional account. Instead, he argues that a free society produces better human beings who, in turn, produce a better society.[10] The tension between individuality and sociality is resolved by demonstrating that neither is really possible without the

---

10. John Stuart Mill, *On Liberty*, esp. chap. 3.

other. But, like Locke and Hobbes, Mill acknowledges the necessity of negative rights, although he is hesitant to label them as such. His harm principle restricts freedom by prohibiting actions that harm others and thereby secures the freedom that allows for human flourishing.

This tension is at the heart of the classical liberal tradition[11] and explains why the enforcement of laws that protect individual rights is so often seen as the primary function of government, perhaps even the only legitimate one. The protection of individual rights is essential to the proper functioning of society. If the government does not do at least this, then society and its attendant benefits simply are not possible. (This is Locke's answer.) Or, to put the point in more Hobbesian terms, it is the creation of a government with the authority to protect each of us from incursions by our fellows that makes rational (as opposed to coercive) interaction among human beings possible to the benefit of all. Or, as Mill might say, the protection of individual rights (the prevention of harm) is essential for the flourishing of both individuals and societies. This tension between individuality and sociality does not present us with a true dilemma, but its resolution requires a deeper understanding of both alternatives. Freedom must be restricted so that sociality can flourish and render the exercise of freedom truly worthwhile; civil authority must be restricted so that individuality can flourish and render authority truly advantageous to all.

DISASTER RELIEF

So . . . is disaster relief more like the protection of individual rights that define a broad sphere of freedom, an essential function of civil

---

11. If the reader would like to examine a contemporary discussion of this issue, I can recommend nothing better than Douglas B. Rasmussen and Douglas J. Den Uyl, *Liberty and Nature: An Aristotelian Defense of Liberal Order* (La Salle, Ill.: Open Court, 1991).

society? Or is it more like the war on drugs or the regulation of the economy to produce certain distributional outcomes, which look to the defender of freedom very much like the illegitimate expansion and misuse of civil authority?

The answer to this question is complex; it requires us to consider the characteristics of an event or situation that is properly called a "disaster" and what, exactly, we mean by "relief." It is surely relevant here to note that one feature of disasters, properly so called, is that they often return those whom they beset to something very much like a state of nature. In the disorder that they engender, the conditions that make it reasonable for individuals to respect the rights of others, or to suppose that any great number will in fact do so, are simply destroyed.

Efforts to survive and recover from the disaster may lead to an escalation of violations of individual rights: assault, fraud, looting. There is frequently an increase in violence born of anxiety and insecurity, or merely of opportunity, and directed against targets that have little or nothing to do with the disaster.[12] There is frequently profiteering, attempts to capitalize on the misfortunes of disaster victims. And while profiteering may not be a crime (i.e., a violation of anyone's rights), it certainly ratchets up the hostility of the victims and thereby contributes to the general level of disorder. Under these conditions, civil society may simply become impossible. Disasters frequently leave only the freedom of the state of nature, which is precisely what government is supposed to deliver us from.

Thus, we might well conclude that some sorts of disaster relief, at least, are a natural extension of the government's authority to protect individual rights. It is easy to imagine the sorts of things that

12. Elaine Enarson provides an interesting analysis of the data on domestic violence in "Violence against Women in Disasters," *Violence against Women* 5, no. 7 (1999): 742.

the government might usefully do to restore order, and thus preserve freedom, in the aftermath of a natural disaster: increased and more aggressive police patrols, perhaps with the assistance of the military; curfews and other restrictions on movement and association; restrictions on communication; perhaps even relaxing the requirements of due process and the restrictions on unreasonable search and seizure. The federal government has pursued all of these courses in the past and will doubtless do so again. All involve substantial restrictions on freedom; but all can, in at least some instances, be defended as necessary to restore the conditions that transform the state of nature into civil society.

So disaster relief is not intrinsically incompatible with or inimical to freedom. But here again the slippery slope looms. Sending the national guard to keep order and coordinate initial relief efforts after a hurricane is one thing. Unleashing FEMA to supervise and finance reconstruction is quite another. Using tax revenues or other "public" resources to stave off starvation and exposure in the aftermath of a flood is one thing. Financing and supervising reconstruction, particularly when reconstruction is carried out in such a way as to invite further catastrophes, is another. And it is another thing still when the federal government moves from disaster relief to disaster mitigation or prevention by mandating how we shall prepare; this unleashes the regulatory steamroller of the federal bureaucracy and intrudes into every corner of life. Yet the federal government currently does all these things; relief expands naturally to encompass reconstruction, which quickly gives birth to prevention. Is the slippery slope of disaster relief simply too dangerous?

I suspect that many who are committed to the ideal of a free society are inclined, however regretfully, to answer this question with a simple affirmative. However, several other responses suggest themselves. First, one might explore the potential for market or other voluntaristic responses to disaster and insist that this potential not be stifled by government responses. Perhaps the descent down the slippery slope can be halted by authorizing government to intervene only when there is no alternative. It is certainly true that the market and the nonprofit sector contribute much to disaster relief already. These contributions range from compiling and disseminating information that enables people and communities to mitigate the effects of disasters to emergency relief to financial and other kinds of help during reconstruction. And there is little doubt that the private sector could and would do considerably more if the role of the federal government were reduced. However, I am not sanguine about this approach. Urbanization has combined with rising expectations to push the economic costs of many natural disasters to levels that beggar even the resources of the insurance industry, not to mention those of private relief organizations.[13] Many insurance companies have simply ceased to offer various kinds of disaster coverage or have raised the premiums well beyond what the consumers will (or even can) pay. The resources of private relief organizations are often not even adequate to the task of providing immediate relief, much less reconstruction. Furthermore, mistrust of the private sector, and particularly the market, leads people to turn to government as a first rather than a last resort. There is little reason to suppose that the private sector can or will do much to halt the expansion of the government's authority under the rubric of disaster relief and prevention.

The conclusion that disaster relief is, in some instances, a natural extension of legitimate civil authority also raises a host of "technical" questions that might usefully be considered. What is truly a disaster that destroys the conditions for civil society and calls for action by the government? What, short of trying to restore the *status quo ante* through massive wealth transfers and stringent preventive regulations, is it appropriate for the government to do?

---

13. For a more detailed discussion of this issue, see Comerio, "Paying for the Next Big One," p. 65.

What approaches to relief are least destructive of freedom in both the short and the long term?

Answers to questions such as these would provide at least a philosophical hedge against unlimited expansion and general misuse of the government's authority under the rubric of disaster relief. They would allow the defender of freedom to explain why the government must respond in some instances and, more important, how both the response and the limitations on it are built on the foundations of a free society. But I will leave these questions to another essay and perhaps even to another author. Instead, I will undertake to place the slippery slope of disaster relief in the context of a larger malaise that pervades the political culture of the United States and that renders all such philosophical speculation as the foregoing largely inefficacious.

THE SLIPPERY SLOPE REVISITED

The thought may have occurred to the reader by now that the slippery slope of disaster relief really is not all that much more slippery or dangerous than that of welfare or economic regulation or universal medical insurance coverage or any of the other myriad programs of the federal government. The federal government has for a long time now been expanding its authority to encompass virtually every aspect of life, with the full support of much of the citizenry. That it should undertake to manage emergencies is not surprising, nor is it even particularly worrisome in the face of this general expansion.

This headlong rush by the citizenry away from freedom and down the road to serfdom is, of course, a complex phenomenon, the product of many factors. But I think that two of these factors are particularly worthy of discussion, one because it is too seldom mentioned and the other because it bears particularly on the issue of disaster relief.

Americans (and perhaps the citizens of other nations as well, although I do not assert this) do not want freedom. Really, they don't. Despite continual and often strident invocation of the ideals of freedom that undergird the political culture and traditions of the United States, the citizens generally do not have any real concern for freedom. What do they want? Lots of things. Some want to smoke marijuana. Some want to build private arsenals. Some want to marry a member of their own sex. Some want to buy cheap gas for their SUVs. Some want their children to pray in school and learn creation science. Many just want to get rich. And some want to prevent others from doing these and other things that they find reprehensible or threatening or offensive or simply pointless. And so on and so on.

My point here is not that these desires and the values they reflect are commensurate with one another or even that all of them are legitimate (or that any of them are not). I have intentionally avoided employing the language of "negative" and "positive" rights and freedom in characterizing this feature of American political culture. Although this is a useful distinction, and one that has been effectively employed to illuminate this important shift in the political culture of the United States, it is not essential to my point.

My point is, simply, that in the vocabulary of American political discourse, "freedom" has become more often than not a synonym for "what I want." People don't want freedom. They just want what they want. If the government allows them to get it or, better yet, gives it to them, then they think themselves free.

This is, certainly, a rather pessimistic view of things, and it is largely impressionistic. But the impressions seem to me utterly compelling. In letters to the editor, and in the ostensibly more thoughtful essays of the pundits, people demand whatever they want as a matter of right and castigate those who want something else. What *I* want is simply to exercise the freedom guaranteed by the Constitution and the traditions of this free country; what *you* want is special privileges at the expense of the common good or a perversion of freedom or whatever. In the debates that surround the controversies of the day—abortion, welfare, environmental degradation, capital punishment—all are the defenders of the rights that constitute our freedom, and their opponents are the enemies of these rights. And our political leaders pander to this confusion, invoking freedom to justify their constituents' demands and promising all sorts of restrictions on the freedom of others. This narcissism is the triumph of individuality over sociality.

The freedom to "order their actions and dispose of their possessions and persons as they think fit, within the bounds of the law of nature, without asking leave or depending upon the will of any other man," is no longer enough for far too many of us. This kind of freedom is hard, and it entails responsibility, which is harder still. Rather, we demand to live in a world that mirrors precisely our values and prejudices and guarantees the fullest satisfaction of our desires; that is to say, we demand freedom from hardship, uncertainty, doubt, confusion. Anything short of this—any necessity that we coexist with others whose values and desires are different from ours and often in competition with them—is oppression of the worst sort.[14]

Bastiat's distinction between what is *seen* and what is *not seen* is surely relevant here, as well. It is easy to see how the power of government might be used to procure what one wants or to remake the world in one's own image. It is not so easy, apparently, to see that this power might turn against one in the future or that others might have different wants and a different picture of how the world

---

14. I explore some of the causes and consequences of this retreat from freedom in a series of lectures I gave to the Institute of Philosophy of the Russian Academy of Sciences. The texts of these lectures are posted on my website (ahrens.hanover.edu/mss). See particularly "The Classical Liberal Tradition in U.S. Politics" and "Divided Self—Divided World: A Call for the Reconstruction of Liberalism."

should be. Bastiat offers an observation about human nature that does much to explain this blindness.

> But there is also another tendency that is common among people. When they can, they wish to live and prosper at the expense of others. This is no rash accusation. Nor does it come from a gloomy and uncharitable spirit. The annals of history bear witness to the truth of it: the incessant wars, mass migrations, religious persecutions, universal slavery, dishonesty in commerce, and monopolies. This fatal desire has its origin in the very nature of man—in that primitive, universal, and insuppressible instinct that impels him to satisfy his desires with the least possible pain.[15]

People want what they want, and what they want most is the security of a guarantee that they will get it. If this comes at the expense of their own freedom or the freedom of others, so be it.

One dimension of this narcissism is an inability to empathize with others, to really imagine what it would be like to have values and desires different from the ones we actually have or to understand the world differently from the way we do. I see the seeds of this malaise every time I raise controversial issues with the students in my classes on ethics and political philosophy. Far too many of them simply cannot imagine what it would be like to have different values and desires—to be attracted to someone of the same sex, to prefer literature to sports (or sports to literature), to believe (or not to believe) in the God of Christianity.

Such values and desires are, quite literally for many of my students, inconceivable; they are not natural, and those who act on them are quite obviously abusing their freedom. Far too many of them simply cannot imagine that they might understand their world and their prospects differently if they had had different experiences, different opportunities, different abilities—in short, dif-

15. Frederic Bastiat, *The Law*, Dean Russell, trans. (Irvington-on-Hudson, N.Y.: Foundation for Economic Education, 1998).

ferent lives. Someone who views the world differently is, at best, mistaken and so obviously mistaken that one is inclined to suspect hypocrisy.

Yet the presence of empathy does not seem to improve the situation much. In the contemporary political culture of the United States, empathic identification with others often simply expands the *I* that demands satisfaction and culminates in the demonization of those who dissent from our views. Those who demand abortion rights are "murderers" and perpetrators of a "holocaust" in the eyes of those who have taken the interests of the "unborn" to heart. Those who question affirmative action are "racist" in the eyes of those who have taken the interests of minorities to heart. Those who promote the improvement of the material conditions of human life are "raping" the environment in the eyes of those who look after the interests of "humanity" or "nature." And so on and on through many of the issues that are the subject of public discourse.

There may be moral absolutes that justify some or all of these charges. And some of these absolutes may be so compelling that they justify the demand that government enforce them. I have certainly argued that the preservation of civil society and the protection of individual rights justify such a demand. In any case, my point is that the tendency to demonize those who disagree with us—to see all disagreements as stark conflicts between good and evil—makes it difficult to discern any value in individual freedom. Freedom comes to be seen as nothing but an excuse to do evil. An empathic identification with the values and perspectives of others too often leads not to an appreciation of the importance of freedom but to a greater insistence that freedom not be allowed to hamper the realization of our values.

The sheer perversity of this shift in the political culture of the United States was brought home to me by experiences in Russia. My first visit to that benighted place in 1990, when the Soviet regime was still in power, confirmed my deepest convictions about the connection between freedom and human flourishing: nothing worked—not the elevators, or the retail system, or the phones, or most of the people—nothing, and no one seemed willing or able to do anything about it. But change was in the air; the Russian people seemed determined to cast off the chains they had forged for themselves and avail themselves of the advantages of freedom.

When I returned several years later, something very much different was in the air. What remained of the old authoritarian political system was largely impotent, giving people freedom of speech and the press and association and religion, and all the political turmoil that these engender, more or less by default. Capitalism, albeit a rather corrupt form of it, had spread like a weed; there were fortunes to be made, and significant opportunities for improving one's standard of living, but there were no guarantees that anyone would succeed or that patterns of economic success and failure would conform to any particular conception of virtue or desert. And everywhere people were beginning to lament the passing of the old regime.

Even those old enough to have lived under Stalin waxed nostalgic: we didn't have much, they were wont to say, but at least we were secure in what we had. This nostalgia for a security that was surely more illusory than real confirms our worst suspicions about the effect of authoritarian regimes on the human spirit; individuality can be so suppressed that freedom comes to seem like nothing more than a threat to security. And this makes our own demands for security at any cost appear all the more pathetic, and even perverse, in that we make these demands not as a hedge against the uncertainties of freedom but in the very name of freedom.

This screed may seem nothing more than a digression, even a hysterical digression, from the central topic of this chapter. Hysterical it may be, but it is no digression. This retreat from freedom is a powerful engine driving the expansion of government, whether it be into emergency management or into some other area of life. This narcissism will ensure that there is a vocal constituency for any expansion of the government's authority that promises to benefit any substantial number of people. And it effectively silences anyone who would resist the expansion of the government's authority in the name of preserving freedom.

If freedom is nothing but "what I want," how can it possibly weigh heavily in the balance against the plight of disaster victims or justice for the victims of discrimination or the safety of consumers? Who but the most depraved wretch could demand freedom if it would hamper the efforts of the government to respond to the many pressing needs of the citizenry? And ultimately, of course, I do not think my screed is at all hysterical. Resisting the expansion of government in the name of freedom is simply no longer respectable among a large segment of the citizenry. And no wonder.

If freedom is just narcissism masquerading as a political philosophy, then freedom itself is not respectable. This is what I meant when I wrote, at the end of the preceding section, that philosophical speculation about freedom is largely inefficacious. Too many people just do not want to hear it. The prospects for freedom are dim; perhaps a bit of hysteria is justified.

UNMAKING VIRTUOUS PERSONS

My second point about the slippery slope of disaster relief can be made with somewhat more brevity and, I hope, somewhat less stridency. Numerous philosophers over the centuries have taken up the issue of whether or not the government is an appropriate tool for making virtuous persons. Those in the classical liberal tradition have typically argued that it is not and, moreover, that the expansion of government's authority is likely to undermine the virtue of citizens. Disaster relief illustrates this point quite nicely. As the government expands its emergency management efforts to include relief, reconstruction, and prevention, the incentives that individuals have to take responsibility for their own protection are correspondingly diminished and likewise the incentives that individuals have to respond in any substantial way to the plight of others who are beset by a disaster. This becomes the government's job; energy and resources that people might devote to doing it themselves get redirected into efforts to ensure that the government does it well. Or the matter is simply ignored until one's own life is ravaged by a disaster. And the expansion of the government's authority has very much the effect of an addictive drug; the more we get, the more we need.

As freedom is diminished, so are the opportunities and incentives for virtues like responsibility, prudence, generosity, and courage. And as the scope and effect of these virtues are diminished, they weigh less and less in the balance against the urgent demands of disaster victims. This effect is certainly not unique to the expansion of the government's authority to respond to natural disasters; it follows on all such expansions. But this unmaking of virtue is exacerbated in the case of natural disasters because these disasters have about them an air of randomness. They seem to strike without warning, to beset responsible and irresponsible people alike, and to destroy the very means by which the victims might make their own recovery.

There seems to be precious little that individuals, or even communities, can do to protect themselves, and this little is very costly. Of course, it isn't strictly true that natural disasters strike without warning: earthquake faults and potential fire zones are well known; rivers flood at fairly predictable frequencies and levels; certain areas of the country are known to be especially vulnerable to tornadoes or hurricanes. And it is not strictly true that disasters strike responsible and irresponsible people alike or that they must deprive people of the means of recovery; people can take all sorts of measures to mitigate the effects of disasters that do strike and to prepare for recovery, although many of these measures are indeed quite costly.

Nonetheless, there is a kernel of truth in this perception of randomness that allows it to overpower alternative views. People choose to live in floodplains or tornado zones because that's where the farmlands are. People choose to live along fault lines because that's where the cities are, with the hubs of communication, transportation, and production that comprise modern enterprise. People chose to live along coastlines threatened by hurricanes because that's where the fisheries and ports and tourists are.

Government is constituted to protect our freedom and thereby facilitate cooperation in the production of the advantages of life; it is the very success of this cooperation that draws more and more people into areas and activities that increase their vulnerability to disasters. They are doing society's work, the work for which society is constituted. Again, it seems that some level of disaster relief is a natural expansion of the authority of government. And, again, it is no surprise that efforts to control this expansion are largely unsuccessful.

The rejection of freedom is of a piece with the rejection of virtue. One can hardly exist without the other, and if it does, it is hard to discern its value. The defenders of freedom may insist that we must restrict the government's authority to manage disasters in order to preserve virtue. But if freedom is not valued, virtue will not be much valued either. It will certainly not outweigh the urgency of rectifying the "unfairness" of nature.

CONCLUSION

It may seem that we have accomplished nothing, that the effort to link disaster relief to the legitimate functions of government in a free society is a fool's errand after all. For I have argued that disaster relief is indeed one of the legitimate functions of government in a free society but also that it poses the same dangers and thus calls for the same strict limitations as other legitimate functions of government. Thus, the government of a free society can give effect to the natural and laudable human inclination to help those beset by calamities not of their own making; it can, in other words, be an instrument of our virtue as well as our freedom. But it can also be the weapon that destroys both freedom and virtue.

Of course, it is clear to anyone who looks that the federal government already has, on any reasonable account of these limitations, exceeded them by a large measure. And I have argued that the political culture of the United States gives us little cause to be surprised by this and little cause to expect anything better in the near future. What good does it do to link disaster relief to freedom when too few people care about freedom for this linkage to have any practical effect?

Some good, perhaps. Consider for a moment the two epigrams at the head of this essay. The meaning of P. J. O'Rourke's simile is clear: it is always—*always*—dangerous to give government the authority to regulate our actions or lay claim to our resources, even if it is sometimes necessary to do so. The meaning of Ben Boggs's insistence that FEMA must compensate him for moving himself and his property (a mobile home) out of danger is less clear. The article in which Mr. Boggs is quoted does not report whether he himself holds a federal flood insurance policy; nor does it report whether he would be willing to forgo federal flood insurance in exchange for being left alone.

In any case, Mr. Boggs does not have this latter option. The article reports that FEMA is threatening to penalize all policyholders in Clark County, Indiana, or perhaps even deny them policies, unless Ben Boggs and others like him are made to comply with federal regulations. This is so often the way of government; it expands its authority by conferring on us benefits that we have not asked for and then demanding that we accommodate ourselves to them and pay for them. Often the benefits are real, which makes Mr. Boggs and others like him appear to be nothing more than cranks.

Perhaps they are cranks. Who but a crank, after all, would insist on parking an expensive mobile home on a floodplain, even if it means depriving his neighbors of the insurance protection they need. But perhaps they are simply people who prefer looking after their own interests to relying on a paternalistic government.

The conflict between Mr. Boggs and FEMA is just an instance of the larger conflict between those who would give government virtually unlimited authority to manage emergencies and those who would limit this authority in order to preserve freedom. And this forces us to confront the question that haunts every effort to defend the ideal of a free society that is preserved by a limited civil authority. Can the government of a free society actually govern? That is, can government act effectively to preserve the structure of rights that make it reasonable for human beings to cooperate in producing the advantages of life without overstepping its boundaries and undoing freedom.

The line of thought I have pursued in this chapter leads me to answer this question in the affirmative, but with an important qualification. The government of a free society can govern effectively without destroying freedom but only if the citizens are willing to be so governed. Mr. Boggs may be a crank. Or he may be a hero of freedom. In the absence of any widespread commitment to freedom, and in light of the sad state of public discourse about the value and scope of freedom, it is difficult to tell.

CHAPTER FOUR

Liberty,
Policy, and
Natural Disasters

Aeon J. Skoble

I

How might a regime of individual liberty handle various destructive natural phenomena, such as earthquakes, floods, or hurricanes? This question seems like the sort of challenge one might make to a defender of liberty, someone who may have argued that the state is not necessary for dealing with such problems. Note that the question presupposes that the state does in fact respond to these catastrophes. When a president or governor declares some scene of major destruction a disaster area, she or he is not merely stating the obvious—the official designation of "disaster area" makes the affected area eligible for various sorts of relief aid. There is a Federal Emergency Management Agency. Like operation of the military, the police, and the court system, coping with natural disasters has in fact been a traditional role of the government. So the defender of the sort of political theory in which the state's role is to be vastly diminished (or eliminated entirely) will typically be expected to explain how such a society would handle natural emergencies.

But among the other presuppositions of the question are, first, that the state does an effective enough job of responding that the burden of proof falls to the libertarian and, second, that "handling" is a simple matter of bringing resources to bear on the problem effectively. Often, the state's performance of some limited function evolves into a massive bureaucracy devoted as much to itself as to its object. Need it be the case with disaster relief as well? By way of answering the initial question, I shall endeavor to address these other presuppositions and side issues.

A common complaint against the state is that bureaucracies devoted to a specific problem have a tendency to work for their own self-preservation. For example, many critics have argued that the bureaucracy of the welfare state designs antipoverty programs that keep a certain percentage of the people poor, so that there will always be someone to help. But regardless of whether this is a valid charge, in an important sense the analogy does not apply to disaster relief, namely, that government bureaucrats do not literally *cause* earthquakes and hurricanes.

However, there *is* a sense in which government agencies do cause damage. Since there is institutionalized, government-subsidized disaster relief and flood insurance, coastal property in hurricane threat zones has become much more developed, with the result that, when hurricanes hit, there are more buildings to destroy than there would likely be if private insurance companies were entirely responsible for these properties (this conundrum will be addressed below). "The broader problem [with the seeming need for government disaster relief] is that many property owners living in disaster-prone areas would probably choose not to insure against catastrophe risks if faced with actuarially fair premiums . . . [so] many people would end up without insurance."[1] This creates, in

---

1. David A. Moss, "Courting Disaster? The Transformation of Federal Disaster Policy since 1803," in *The Financing of Catastrophe Risk*, ed. Kenneth A. Froot (Chicago: University of Chicago Press, 1999), p. 344.

turn, a greater demand for government involvement in disaster relief.

The circularity here is especially vicious: government disaster insurance and relief make it easier to choose to live in a risky area, but the increased number of people at risk make government disaster programs more indispensable. If there were no special incentives to place oneself at risk, fewer people would, and there would be less disaster relief needed. So, clearly, a society that prioritized liberty would have fewer problems of that sort. Nevertheless, it is true that there would still be natural disasters even without the government and true that any society, even a maximally libertarian one, would need to have some mechanism for handling the problems that would arise as a result.

What does it mean to "handle" these sorts of problems? For the most part, it *doesn't* mean prevention. Again, since we are talking about natural disasters, to a large extent we must simply accept the fact that they will happen. In this context, it only means dealing with the aftermath of the phenomena, which means helping people medically, helping people financially, and cleaning up the damage. Understood this way, disaster relief is matter of concentrating resources on a particular region or specific set of victims.

This is sometimes known as a "collective action problem," "collective" because it often entails the coordination of resources from large numbers of people, "problem" because there needs to be some organized way to coordinate the actions or donations so they are properly directed. How is this collective action problem different from others? One, it needs to be immediate. When a hurricane has left 150 people homeless, a five-year plan fails to address the problem. Two, it is supposed to be temporary, a discrete response to a particular event. Once the people (say) have new homes, the emergency is over.

Several liberty concerns arise as a result of all this. First of all, is society's need to respond to this sort of situation an argument in favor of the state? Can these problems be addressed without the state? Second, does the state exploit its current role in this matter to expand the scope of its authority beyond its original justification? These are the key issues that remain.

II

It seems odd to suggest that state action is the only way to address a problem (in this chapter, I am not bothering with the U.S.-specific distinction between state governments and the federal government; I am using "state" in the generic political sense). But we grow accustomed to certain matters being the purview of the state, and then it becomes difficult to conceptualize the state not being involved. But our challenged imaginations are not the same thing as an argument.

For example, the government has long been the operator of the postal service, and it is difficult for many people to imagine how they would get mail if there were no post office. But in the past two decades, the vast growth of UPS and Federal Express shows that it is possible for a private company to establish a nationwide system for routing, distribution, and speedy delivery of items.

The conceptual failing is actually largely semantic: people cannot imagine life without the United States Postal Service, but what they are really having trouble conceiving is life without mail. But there's a difference between privatizing the postal system and eliminating the postal system, and no one actually suggests the latter. Similarly, with phone service: anyone over the age of thirty will remember the expression "the phone company." Now a remark involving that phrase would be criticized for vagueness since there are many competing phone companies.

Because there is a demand for telephone service and mail delivery, we can imagine that a free market would provide them, although there will be some argument about whether there should be a regulated or unrestricted market in those services. But what about disaster relief? Would disaster relief also emerge in a free society, or is this an example of "market failure" requiring the intervention of the state? Some argue that there is a moral obligation to aid the needy. If that is so, then government disaster relief would be justified on the grounds that we are all fulfilling our moral obligations when we pay our taxes to support such programs. However, saying that something is justified is not to say that something is necessary.

In other words, the government relief program may be permissible (one way to fulfill our moral duties), but it may not be obligatory (the only way to fulfill our moral duties). So the question need not devolve to one of moral duties. The question would remain how best to discharge those duties. To argue that state action is the only way to meet these duties is to argue that social cooperation requires state intervention.

This is essentially what seventeenth-century philosopher Thomas Hobbes was arguing when he argued for the necessity of an absolute sovereign. Without a centralized authority to "keep us in awe," the argument goes, we would not be able to cooperate on even as simple a task as maintaining the peace. Since it is paradigmatically in our own best interests not to have all others trying to kill us, a version of Hobbes's argument tends to be invoked whenever the issue of social cooperation arises. If we can't even cooperate at the minimal level needed to secure peace, why should we be able to cooperate on more complex tasks such as educating the young or feeding the poor or building roads or responding to natural disasters?

The problem with this line of reasoning is that the initial premise is mistaken. Ample research demonstrates that cooperation can arise independently of state intervention. For instance, decision theorist Robert Axelrod's now-famous computer simulation showed conclusively that cooperation was the strategy that produced the best outcomes over the long term.[2] It was actually a certain kind of cooperation that was most robust, a responsive approach to cooperation that tries to encourage others to cooperate but is capable of punishing them if they refuse. Subsequent research (e.g., by Martin Nowak and Karl Sigmund[3]) has confirmed that, even assuming the most self-interested motivations, cooperation can develop naturally. So since the argument that government intervention is necessary to ensure that people will cooperate fails in general, it cannot be invoked as a rationale for the necessity of the state for the coordination of disaster relief efforts.[4]

So how are the relief efforts to be coordinated in a free society?

In times past, charity was typically handled through private means: religious groups, mutual aid societies, and philanthropic millionaires. In the newsletter of the Capital Research Center, Daniel Oliver has documented how, for example, the city of Chicago was rebuilt after the 1871 fire almost entirely through nongovernmental charitable initiatives.[5] Plainly, it is at least possible that disasters could be dealt with independently of the government. So it would seem as though the state is not necessary, at least in the strict sense: if any disaster has been responded to effectively by private means, then it is false that the state is necessary for disaster relief.

Nevertheless, one would hope for a more interesting answer: in

2. Robert Axelrod, *The Evolution of Cooperation* (New York: Basic Books 1984).

3. Martin Nowak and Karl Sigmund, "A Strategy of Win-Stay, Lose-Shift that Outperforms Tit-for-Tat in the Prisoner's Dilemma Game," *Nature* 364 (July 1, 1993).

4. I explore the fuller political ramifications of this argument in "The Anarchism Controversy," in *Liberty for the 21st Century*, ed. Machan and Rasmussen (Lanham, Md.: Rowman and Littlefield, 1995), and in greater depth in the forthcoming monograph *Freedom, Authority, and Social Order*.

5. Daniel T. Oliver, "Helping the Needy: Lessons from the Chicago Fire," Capital Research Center Newsletter, July 1999.

today's world, is it necessary that the government operate disaster relief activities as it does? Again, the status quo influences one's reactions to such a question. Since the state in fact does assume the service of disaster relief, we come to think of that as a fundamental task of the government, perhaps even a defining one. Even people who might be sympathetic to the claim that the government should be limited will regard certain functions of the state as essential—for example, operating an army.

Disaster relief may well have taken on that appearance. Indeed, in the modern world, the more visible the state's role in disaster relief, the more likely people will be to see it as a fundamental: when we turn on TV news reports about how a catastrophe is being handled, we are most likely to remember the well-organized efforts of a National Guard unit that had been mobilized to respond. Of course, we also see pictures of private citizens pitching in to help their community voluntarily, but these are often judged less cameraworthy.

But here is another circularity: one motivation for joining the National Guard is so that you will be able to help out your community in case of emergency. So the presence of a state-run disaster relief machinery absorbs much of whatever volunteerism there is regarding such activities. Then it becomes difficult to conceptualize people having the means to help if it weren't for the state. Michael Taylor explains that

> the more the state intervenes . . . , the more "necessary" (on this view) it becomes, because positive altruism and voluntary cooperative behavior *atrophy* in the presence of the state and *grow* in its absence. Thus, again, the state exacerbates the conditions which are supposed to make it necessary.[6]

Because the state takes upon itself various duties, Taylor argues,

6. Michael Taylor, *The Possibility of Cooperation* (London: Cambridge University Press 1987), p. 168.

individuals not only lose opportunities to cooperate for various ends, they lose the interest. "[The citizen] may come to feel that his responsibility to society has been discharged as soon as he has paid his taxes (which are taken coercively from him by the state). . . . The state releases the individual from the responsibility or need to cooperate with others directly."[7]

So the question is not so much whether the private sector can do things the state cannot but whether the state's presence has a negative effect on individual incentive to help others.

Of course, another incentive for joining the National Guard is that it pays. These same people, presumably, could be enticed to work in a similar capacity by a private disaster relief agency. But that merely pushes the question back one level. The state agencies get their funding through taxes, which is to say they get funding without regard to demand for their services or ability to deliver results. A private agency would have to either be staffed by volunteers or get its money from people willing to pay, who would have to either be philanthropists or people paying for something they valued. Would people be interested in responding, through labor or money, to an emergency?

It seems reasonable to suspect that people would be willing to respond to emergencies that affect them—for instance, cleaning up their town after it has been flooded. But people may have less of an interest in helping communities more remote from their experience or may be willing to help but literally unable if, for instance, the damage is more severe than the people have the resources to deal with. These seem like the underlying concerns that might be taken to justify the state's involvement: the former is a variation on the traditional "market-failure" argument for state intervention, and the latter is a straightforward allocation-of-resources situation.

7. Ibid., p. 169.

III

Is there good reason to think that there is sufficiently little social cooperation, even regarding helping out in an emergency, as to amount to "market failure"? By "market failure" in the context of social cooperation, especially in emergency situations, we must be referring to something like "an insufficient amount of people willing to devote resources to help respond to emergencies." For example, it is often said that "nonexcludable" public goods such as lighthouses would not get built in a free market because the threat of free-riders would be a substantial disincentive to the providers. (Of course, lighthouses *were* built by the private sector, but the persistence of this argument is as strong as a cold virus.) Therefore, government action is needed to ensure that the goods are provided despite the market failure. If the good is needed, but not enough people are willing to pay for it, it will not appear. So since there is a general need, the government provides the good using tax money.

Disaster relief might be thought of in these terms: everyone would like to see the hurricane-ravaged town rebuilt, but no one seems willing to put up enough money to fund it, so the government has to step in.

Is it true that, left to their own devices, people would not be willing to help each other when there has been a flood or hurricane in their community? This seems implausible. But it is possible that a community may be so devastated that it is incapable of helping itself and requires assistance from outside the community. Would anyone from outside the affected community be willing to help? That would be an empirical matter: clearly some people would be and others less so.

It is hard to forecast the percentages because, first, every emergency is different and, second, some of the willingness to help has been siphoned off by things like the National Guard having already attracted a large portion of those who would be willing to help and taxes having been collected to pay for federal disaster relief programs. This is a considerable factor in gauging people's willingness to help. If I am forced to pay to contribute to government disaster relief efforts, I may feel that I've already "done my part" when the call goes out for help. If the government is inefficient about allocating the taxed resources, and cannot afford to respond adequately, then there will be a need for more help; but many people will refuse ("I gave at the office"), and this would be a second sense in which the government's attempts to coordinate disaster relief end up making things worse.

It also depends on how "community" is conceived. The more localized the community is, the more likely people are to feel an imperative to lend a hand. If one's own town, or even the next town over ("my neighbors"), is flooded or blown away by a hurricane, it is not easy to imagine people refusing to help, especially because in one sense, altruism and self-interest nearly coincide. Each person in the town has a clear interest in rebuilding the town, an interest that cannot be neatly categorized as self-interest or altruism. It may be Jim's Coffee Shop, but I eat there every day. The more remote the disaster, the less likely this sentiment seems to be: someone in Idaho may not feel as compelled to help rebuild a hurricane-ravaged town in Florida, since that isn't in any recognizable sense part of the same community. It is, of course, part of the nation, but that is an artificial distinction to some extent.

To people in, say, northern Idaho, neighboring Canadians may be felt to be more a part of the community than the more remote, albeit politically related, Floridians are. Some Idahoans may, of course, want to help the Floridians out of pure sympathy. Some may be motivated by a self-interest; for instance, a lumber mill owner may see an opportunity for bulk sales and offer cheap prices.

There are also more complex mixes of altruism and self-interest. In a recent television commercial, Miller Beer reminds us of the time when some southern town was flooded, and Miller sent in truckloads of drinking water, bottled in beer bottles after it had retooled the brewery. This cannot be interpreted categorically as altruism, since Miller derives valuable public relations and good will from the act and the continued retelling of the act on TV (message: we care). But neither can it be interpreted as narrowly self-interested as there are cheaper ways to advertise, and it's entirely plausible that some Miller executives genuinely felt they should help in this way. Examples like this one demonstrate that the categories of altruism and self-interest do not always do the work they are supposed to.

It's not a clean dichotomy between looking to help others and serving my own interests exclusively. One can have a self-interest in helping another, or one can simultaneously benefit oneself and another, or one can have feelings of sympathy that do not contradict self-regard. In fact, people seem to manifest these different traits precisely in emergency situations: we all have to pitch in to save the town. Is that helping the community or helping myself? Again, if I perceive it as my town, my community, then I can easily be motivated to help. But this brings us back to the question of the definition of community in a twofold way.

First, what is the scope, and, second, who decides? As to the first dimension, the scope of the community, for most people there seems to be a vaguely defined threshold. The nearer the disaster to the person's experience, the more keenly is felt the need to help. The more remote the disaster, the more likely the person will regard it as someone else's problem, however calamitous. Most of us would gladly offer shelter to our next-door neighbors if their house burned down, but when we hear about an earthquake in Turkey, we typically do not offer to fly people over to stay with us. (The defeater to the geographic threshold condition is, of course, family ties: we would be more likely to want to help a family member or any close friend regardless of distance.)

One argument for government disaster relief would be that it ties together communities that are geographically remote under a common bond, thus enabling people in Idaho to feel more connected to Floridians and facilitating transfers of assistance.

But why should political distinctions be a paramount consideration? If the argument is that one has a moral obligation to help the needy, surely a needy person in Guatemala has as much a claim to that help as a person in Florida. But if the argument is not one of universal moral obligation but of political alliance, then the Floridian has a more tangible claim on our help than the Guatemalan. And this would seem to give rise to the argument for the state's involvement: since we are in a political union, we will all contribute x dollars to a pool of common money for disaster relief, and any community in our union may draw on that fund should there be an emergency. That sounds prudent.

Why, though, should we think that only the state may operate such a fund? Of course, when the state operates the fund, it ceases to be voluntary, and hence the liberty objection: why should I be *forced* to contribute? The nonvoluntary nature of the present arrangement is partly why political means are inefficient. A purely voluntary system of mutual aid would be unlikely to offer cheap assistance to developers of beach property in hurricane zones. If the argument for the state's involvement in disaster relief is that it is an efficient way to coordinate social action, it couldn't be more mistaken.

Another sort of argument for the state's involvement, or perhaps a tacit component of the previous, is that the state's coercive means are necessary because otherwise there just won't be enough assistance to go around. We turn to that argument next.

IV

If we look at disaster relief as a matter of distribution of social resources, we can say either that a free market will address the problem or that it won't, and hence government action is necessary. The former response would require an argument like this: since people want their houses rebuilt or their towns cleaned up, there is a market for the provision of these services, and, hence, absent state interference in the market, they would be provided at a price people chose to pay in accordance with the value they place on them.

But, sound or not, that argument will fail to persuade the very people who find it difficult to conceptualize nongovernmental disaster relief, so perhaps it would be most profitable to examine the facets of the latter response. Say the free market wouldn't adequately allocate resources to respond to the financial hardships of disaster relief. Even given a role for the state in this area, we have two distinct models for government involvement; call them the school paradigm and the food paradigm. On the school paradigm, the reasoning is that, since society has a duty to provide a decent education for all, the state must operate schools. There are three possible objections to this.

First, one could argue that there is no social duty to provide education for others, no obligation for Smith to support the education of Jones's children. Second, one could observe that the inference is logically fallacious, absent a premise equating social action with state action. These objections will go unexamined for the present discussion. But a third objection one might make is that even accepting that there is a social obligation to provide education, it is not clear that operating schools is the best way to do this. One alternative possibility would be on what I have called the food paradigm. If there is anything more essential to life than education, it would surely be food, and anyone who agrees that there is a social obligation to make sure everyone is educated is likely to agree also that everyone should be fed. Yet the model for state action here is wholly different.

No one today seriously argues that the state should run farms and operate supermarkets. Countries that do still operate this way are plagued by shortages, whereas our current system produces an overabundance. It is commonly acknowledged that our current system is the most efficient way to produce and distribute food, although some people are so poor that they cannot afford sufficient food. But the mechanism for social assistance for such people is to enable them to afford it through direct cash payments or food stamps.

One advantage of the food paradigm over the school paradigm is that the former recognizes the superior efficiency of the free market in production and distribution, while responding to social concerns about poverty, whereas the latter responds to those concerns in a way which, in an effort to avoid the social costs of the market, eliminates the benefits as well. Even given statist presuppositions, the food paradigm is clearly the more efficient model of the two. Which should be the operative model for disaster relief should be evident. If the argument for government involvement in disaster relief is a concern that people simply cannot afford to help themselves, then the solution is direct cash payments, rather than an institutionalized bureaucracy, which, as we have seen, indirectly exacerbates the very problems it is intended to address.

If there were no government disaster relief, what would be the alternatives? Certainly there would be private charitable agencies, such as the Red Cross or the United Way. If people weren't currently taxed to pay for disaster relief, they would have to assume personal responsibility for contributing, and the result would be variable: one imagines that some would contribute more than they pay under the current system but that others would contribute less.

Given other reductions of the scope of government, we might see more entrepreneurial mixtures of altruism and self-interest, such as a foreign corporation seeking to establish goodwill might follow the lead of Miller Beer, providing or underwriting assistance in return for the public relations benefit. Ultimately, of course, it is impossible to predict exactly what sorts of institutions might arise to respond to such emergencies. There may be a role for emergency cash transfer payments but not for an institutionalized government presence. The argument that disasters could not possibly be addressed without the state's intervention is false since historical examples to the contrary abound, and the argument that the state is the most efficient way to coordinate resources is flawed for the reasons I have tried to elaborate here.

What if the worst is true? What if a free society turned out to be incapable of responding adequately to these disasters? It seems reasonable to want an answer to this question. But first, let's think about what such a question means.

Again, it partly depends on how we define "adequate response." That seems to mean "efficiently and effectively coordinate the provision of relief services." We have seen that there is no reason to think that a nongovernmental organization could not do this, and some reason to think that government involvement makes things worse. But, for the sake of argument, if this analysis were wrong, what would that imply about the scope of government authority? Less than the statist might think.

It might justify the existence of a government mechanism for coordination of relief efforts without justifying the provision of those efforts. It might justify the provision of relief only in those cases where the private efforts are inadequate. It might justify temporary, ad hoc, deployment of resources without justifying a large institutionalized structure. This last observation speaks to the responsibility issue, which needs revisiting. Of all the problems one can point to in a bureaucratized disaster relief system, the most dangerous, and the most clearly identifiable as unjustified, is the way in which state-sponsored disaster insurance creates an incentive to develop property in known potential disaster areas like hurricane zones and floodplains. The erosion of personal responsibility this engenders is the reductio ad absurdum of this pattern.

Conservative and libertarian critics of the welfare state have long argued that the fact that the state makes it more attractive to not work than to work at a low-wage job creates a sense that people are not responsible for their own upkeep (Charles Murray, to take one example).[8] The state will look after them. Whether this is apt or not, it is plain that federally subsidized flood insurance and the like give people an incentive to build and develop in places they otherwise would not. Oceanfront lots, for example, are very attractive to people who like the ocean. But one generally wants to insure such an investment.

Insurance companies base their premiums on the information they can gather about similar things, "similar" because although each case is different, one can extrapolate statistically from trends and probabilities. For example, health insurance premiums may be more expensive for a smoker, not because the insurance company knows that *this person* will incur greater medical expenses but because smokers tend to. Auto insurance premiums are higher if you own a late-model car and live in New York City, not because they know that *your car* will be stolen but because there is a demonstrable rate of thefts of certain models.

So in these two cases, statistically, it is more of a risk to insure you even though each individual case is unpredictable, and the insurance companies reflect that enhanced risk in their rate structure. You can get insurance despite the risk; it is simply going to cost more. Now a geographic area may also have demonstrable patterns—for example, the chance of your home being damaged by an earthquake is greater if you live in San Francisco, or New Madrid, Missouri, than if you live in Manhattan, although the burglary rate may be higher in Manhattan. So in Manhattan you would expect to pay more for theft insurance but less for earthquake insurance. (No one is currently proposing that there be federally subsidized theft insurance for city dwellers.)

8. Charles Murray, *Losing Ground* (New York: Basic Books, 1984).

Similarly, your hurricane insurance will likely be less than if you lived in South Florida or along the Carolina coast. In a purely free society, of course, people would be free to live on the Carolina coast or in New Madrid, but it would be up to them to bear the cost of the higher insurance premiums. Currently, a variety of government programs make it more attractive to assume these risks than they otherwise would be. Federal flood insurance, for example, is available to those people who live in communities that participate in the National Flood Insurance Program. Although payouts do not come directly from tax dollars, the rates are lower because of the pooled risk of the participating communities.[9] (This sort of pooled risk could be coordinated by any large insurance concern, so the question is whether the government runs it because it is so unprofitable that no insurance company wants to or whether the government runs it because it is assumed to be the only organization capable of doing so.)

To the extent that the cost of bearing an increased risk is artificially reduced, people will come to see greater incentive in assuming that risk. People are actually encouraged to incur greater risks and then are eligible for assistance when the worst comes to pass. When one suffers automobile damage, one's car insurance rates rise, on the theory that this is evidence that your risk is somewhat higher than the norm. But if one is a flood victim, one may continue to reside in the risky area at a cost that does not reflect this because of the cost-pooling arrangements of the NFIP.

Communitarians would likely endorse the notion that, since we are all part of the community, we all have an obligation to help people afford housing and help victims of natural disasters. One slogan of the communitarian movement, though, is "rights *and*

---

9. For a fuller discussion of the National Flood Insurance Program and its social cost, see "The Role of Government in Responding to Natural Catastrophes" by N. Scott Arnold, in this volume.

responsibilities."[10] Naturally one has the right to live in a flood hazard area or a hurricane zone, but one should also have the responsibility to bear the increased risks involved. The government's subsidizing the assumption of higher risk entails an erosion of personal responsibility, which then feeds into the notion that the government is necessary to help people. The impression is that the government is needed to help people who are in trouble as a result of its own policies.

V

What can we conclude? It seems as though the government is not *necessary* for the provision of disaster relief, that there is every reason to think that a libertarian-oriented society would be capable of responding to natural disasters, that extant government disaster programs exacerbate many of the problems they are meant to alleviate, and that these programs have a tendency to erode personal responsibility. They erode responsibility both in those who are encouraged to assume risks they otherwise would not and, ironically, in those who help others less than they otherwise would because they have come to think that the government will take care of it.

Like so many government programs, the government disaster apparatus entails dramatic countervailing effects that undermine its legitimacy yet is firmly entrenched both in terms of the public perception and in terms of the self-preservation instincts of all bureaucracies. What can be done? It would seem politically unfeasible to simply abolish FEMA and its many programs.

Some short-term suggestions, some of which I have alluded to, thus seem appropriate. Other than switching from a schools paradigm to a food paradigm, which is politically no more feasible than abolition, one more interesting, and I think more productive, sug-

10. See, for example, the journal *The Responsive Community*.

gestion would be to alter the mission of FEMA to be one of coordinating, rather than providing, relief. (Perhaps other brewers will compete for the privilege of providing bottled water to stricken towns.) This would allow the bureaucracy to continue to exist but would restore the concept of private provision of emergency assistance to one of voluntary helping with a true sense of community. This would restore some sense of the importance of voluntary assistance in a free society, which communitarians as well as libertarians ought to endorse.

Another short-term modification would be to limit the role of the state in these matters to the truly unexpected. We can know with reasonable certainty that certain regions are likely to be stricken with floods or hurricanes or earthquakes, whereas in other areas it may be completely unexpected, the result of an incredibly unlikely confluence of events or conditions. We could limit the FEMA mission to one of responding to the unpredictable emergencies, rather than the ones that could have been expected. This way, government assistance would be available when the inconceivable happens, but people who want to live in a floodplain or a hurricane zone or on a fault line would be forced to assume their fair share of the risks that that entails. This would address the personal responsibility issue from the other side, while reducing the scope of government involvement.

Both these short-term suggestions would still leave the state apparatus in place, which is not ideal. But these changes might, after a time, bring about a change in public perception and attitude.

There might then come a time when the countervailing effects of government-run disaster relief would be more readily apparent, and there could be sufficient support for privatization. As with other government programs, part of the continued support for federal disaster relief stems from a lack of public awareness of alternatives and of the history of the program. People seem to support programs more firmly when they cannot see how else a problem would be addressed.

The two interim proposals I suggest would provide at least a glimpse of an alternative, opening the door to further discussion about the role of the state.

INDEX